The RAINBOW QUEST

The RAINBOW QUEST

Anuenue in the race for the Transpac Cup

by the best selling author of
Celestial Navigation by HO249

Stu Milligan

The RAINBOW QUEST

by Stu Milligan

United Writers™ is an imprint of
W.E.C. Plant Publishing
ISBN 0913611 SAN 285-3612
Box 61751 Honolulu Hawaii, 96839
E-mail: AlandJulie.Plant@Worldnet.att.net

Technical Production:
Carl Wagner, PCM Computer Services
E-mail: P.C.M.@Worldnet.att.net
Raymond Santana, Express Copy Inc.

First Edition, April, 1997

DEDICATION

To the crew of Anuenue
Vernon Smith, Joe Dolan, Kevin Smith,
Craig Smith, Jorge Rivera
and Photographer Gordon "Gordo" Jay.

And to Nonnie who waited till we came home.

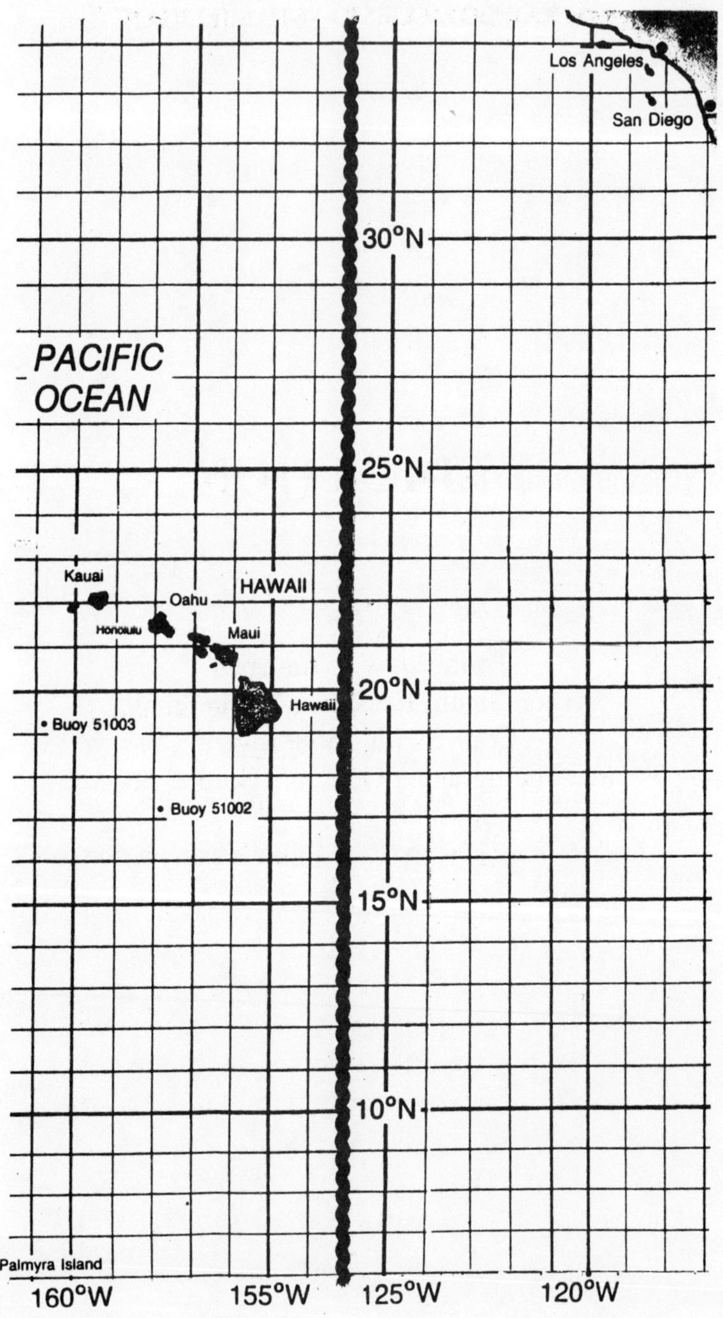

Los Angeles
San Diego
30°N
PACIFIC
OCEAN
25°N
Kauai
Oahu
HAWAII
Honolulu
Maui
20°N
Hawaii
• Buoy 51003
• Buoy 51002
15°N
10°N
Palmyra Island
160°W
155°W
125°W
120°W

PROLOGUE

I signed the document for the inspector from the State Department of Agriculture attesting to the fact that there was no fresh fruit, or other State contraband aboard, and handed it back to him. The Race Committee representative had been awaiting his turn. He stepped forward and handed me a one page document. I scanned it quickly. My signature, and that of my watch captains, would pledge that we had not used our engine during the race, and that we had acquired no private weather information at any time since the start of the race on July fourth. I signed and called Vernon and Joe. They read it, signed and returned it to the representative.

The gala noisy throng, including our families and many of our friends, would now be permitted to come aboard, provided they had proper identification as guests. Our wives had submitted a list to the committee before our arrival naming those they had selected. Without some control we would surely have sunk at our mooring from the sheer weight of numbers.

We were dressed in our Sunday best, as far as yachting costumes go. We had bathed in salt water, trimmed our beards and donned our uniform crew shirts and white shorts before we crossed the finish line. We were, however, a mess. Our decks, cabin, cockpit and our uniforms were plastered with bits of wet red paper. The smell of firecrackers, even though the fresh tradewind was blowing, still clung to *Anuenue* and to us.

There were leis of plumeria, carnation and tuberose piled to our ears. We were crowned with garlands of fern and orchids. A hefty bamboo goblet, brimming over with mai-tai was thrust into my hand. The aroma of hot pupus began steaming up from a cooker on the cabin top, hiding the smell of firecrackers. “Auntie Jeanne” showed up in the nick of time and thrust a quart carton of passion fruit juice at me, to save me from the explosion the mai-tai would surely cause in my dehydrated mid section, if it were not properly wetted down first. I drank the juice heartily, (there was no potable liquid aboard upon our arrival). Now I was ready for the mai-tai and the pupus.

Gone in a flash were the problems of the past thirteen days. A moment of plenty was at hand.

The party was magnificent, and it lasted well into the day. When it was over, all of our guests were gone and *Anuenue* was cleaned up, my wife turned to me and asked, “Well, tell me about the race, how was it?”

“Fine,” I answered, “just fine, a problem here and there, but fine.”

CHAPTER I

HONOLULU, 1969

If there had been a trace of prudence in my make-up, I would surely have answered Vernon with a categorical "NO" when he said to me from across my desk, "So! Let's get our own "41" and race it down anyway." But desire over the years to skipper a boat in the race had proved too strong; any prudence in such a matter had been washed away by wave after wave of downright envy of the skippers who tied up at the Transpac mole after this most glamorous of all races.

The biannual Transpacific race from Point Fermin outside of Los Angeles breakwater to Diamond Head was the one in question. It is run each odd year starting at high noon on July 4th and ending 2,225 miles away, ten days to two weeks later, depending upon the speed of the boat, the force of the wind, the skill of the crew and that most fickle female, Lady Luck.

I should have answered "No." My business, my bank account and my savings were in no condition to be strained to the extent necessary to participate in such a commitment; but weak and captivated as I was insofar as the Transpac was concerned, I answered, "Why not?" and so the commitment was made.

If I could have foreseen even some of the problems that lay ahead, that trace of prudence might have been stirred to life, and reason might have prevailed; but, I don't think so.

It was too easy to just close my eyes and see myself charging majestically down the Molokai Channel, spinnaker drawing, all sheets taut, outmaneuvering the 50 foot Class "B" boat abeam of me and surfing across the finish line first in class, first in fleet, and first Hawaiian boat in years to capture the coveted Governor's trophy and bring it back home where it most rightly belonged. It was just too easy. What I lacked in prudence, I made up in imagination, and I was hooked.

Vernon is my brother-in-law. He was a Ford dealer in the process of selling some of his interest in the business, and he made it all sound so simple and logical, particularly to my preconditioned mind. He wanted some other venture to invest in and the two of us had been talking for sometime about starting a boat business. We had formed a small company and had purchased a Newport 30 sloop. I had taken and passed my Coast Guard tests for a minimum commercial license and we had, in our spare time between races, done some chartering and sailing instruction work with the sloop. We would put company development plans in abeyance; sell the N/30, borrow whatever else was needed, order the N/41, race it down and with all the glory of victory, sell it for a handsome profit. We would then be ready to launch the new boating business from a solid base, our reputation already made. Of course, there was a chance —a slim one— we wouldn't win first overall. We were bound to do well, however. Wasn't the Newport 41 almost a copy of *Red Jacket*? Hadn't *Red Jacket* cleaned up on a number of mainland racing circuits during the past year? Of course she had. And wasn't I a cool one when it came to being a racing skipper? Without a doubt. With the crew we could put together, there was no question. We would do well. So went the reasoning in that flash of time before I answered "Why not?" —cool, careful and calculating.

Having made the main decision, the only one of any real importance, I had some others to consider. My current business venture was the ownership and operation of an executive placement agency. The agency had done fairly well for a couple of years, but was now at a low ebb. Jobs were plentiful, but applicants difficult to find. The employment level was just too high to require my services. The agency wouldn't survive without my time, as I was the only executive interviewer; so, what to do? This decision was easy to make. I decided to close the office.

I had been giving sailing instructions weekends, working with a large marine supply firm located at Kewalo Basin, and I felt sure they could use my services in exchange for that elusive commodity, cash. We agreed, Vernon and I, that I would approach them for employment, and if this resulted in an offer satisfactory to me I would close my office and start to work, with the understanding that I would be away for the race and for a shakedown period prior to it. We would then contact Lindsey Plastics for a price on a Newport 41. There was no decision to be made concerning the boat—this 41 was what we wanted. If everything fell into place up to this point, we would then proposition the bank for the necessary capital to finance the venture.

Much to my surprise, because I still didn't believe it would all work out, things did fall into place. I was employed at terms I could accept, and Lindsey Plastics came back with a satisfactory price. Our banker even said yes. He must have had a weakness or a daydream of his own—which is not unusual for bankers in matters involving the lending of money.

When we turned to making up the order for the boat, we were like youngsters turned loose in a candy store. We spent most of the day with John and Jay Moore, who had each ordered an N/41 for the race. They had already been to Newport, California to see and to sail in one of the first boats out of the mold. We went over the specifications of their draft, and made page after page of paper decisions concerning our own.

She was to be a thing of beauty; mystic blue hull with a dark-blue cove stripe, boot top and bottom. There would be medium blue non-skid on deck laid in a white background. We would have pedestal steering with a Danforth compass in a gleaming stainless steel case. We decided on teak grab rails to run the length of the cabin top, with an internal grab rail from which to cling in a heaving sea.

She was taking on a personality already.

She was to have two clear Plexiglas cabin top hatches, and blue vinyl bunk and cockpit cushions. Her interior liner would be smoke gray and would be accented with natural teak. We would not order a carpet at this time, we would have it made up in Honolulu later after the wear and tear of the Transpac was done with. Her galley would be equipped with a three burner alcohol stove, complete with oven.

(The builders later objected to our decision to use alcohol. They felt that butane suited a yacht of this majestic quality better, but we held fast. The Coast Guard as well as our insurance agent looks with disfavor on heavier than air gasses with a propensity for settling in bilges and thus creating an explosive fire hazard. We had to consider the opinion of inspectors representing such agencies for we might want to use our vessel in a commercial venture of some kind at a later date.)

Running rigging would include two spinnaker halyards; it's a log downwind run from Los Angeles and "back-up" gear is essential. Our halyards would be external. Internal halyards, hidden from the wind and unwelcome entanglement aloft, would be nice, but expensive, and we did have a budget to meet. We would have a double headsail rig for reaching. The staysail halyard would be led through a block three-fourths of the height of the mast from the deck. The sail would tack to a car on a track running down the center of the foredeck. This sail would also serve as a spinnaker staysail. All head sails would sheet through blocks that could be snapped into any desirable location along an anodized aluminum toe rail that would run from bow to stern on each gunwale. From such a block, each sheet would run to large turning blocks located on each quarter and from there to the winches. She would have two big Barlow 28 winches to handle the head sails. There would be two 24's aft of the 28's to handle spinnaker sheets and guys. A 16 and 22 would be located on the cabin top for main sheet and other cockpit duty and three 16's would be mounted on the mast to make certain that halyards were up taut.

In the cockpit there would be an electronic wind guide so that the helmsman could see at a glance from whence cometh the breeze that blows us steadily onward. There would be a Signet knot meter so we would know, "Oh! how swiftly," she moves along, and a log so that we may read at any moment how far behind falls Catalina and, of course, the rest of the fleet.

For auxiliary power, we chose gasoline instead of diesel. We saved a thousand dollars and several hundred pounds with this decision. Pounds must be taken into consideration for, after all, the wind must push the weight through the water and every one that can be saved adds a bit of speed for the long sail home. For the same reason, we elected to omit the refrigeration unit from our ice chest. The unit could be installed later in Honolulu.

We made these and many other decisions throughout the afternoon and when we were finished we were certain that we had ordered a thing not only of beauty, but of power and grace as well. The personality she had acquired as she was being created in our minds now required a name.

A two family conference was called to consider this most important question. Her name must be Hawaiian, we decided, for wasn't she destined to bring back a title to this, her homeland? We consulted the Hawaiian dictionary, studied its pages and reached our decision. She would be called *Anuenue*—Rainbow—for her beauty and to symbolize the good fortune she would bring.

Anuenue would need sails. She must have a wardrobe of finery that would suit every occasion she would meet from her start on July 4th until she crossed the finish line off Diamond Head.

Aboard the Newport 30 we had been carrying a 150% genoa with which I was particularly pleased. It had the shape that a driving head sail should have with the fullness forward and smoothing off to an ever flattening run to the leach. We had a successful year with the '30, spending more time out in front of our competition than somewhere back in the pack, and I attributed a good part of this success to the effectiveness of the genoa. The sail carried the label of Baxter and Cicero, Newport Beach, California. They must create the wardrobe for Anuenue.

I drafted a letter to the firm outlining my interests in general and asking for advise on sail inventory, cloth weights, cut, etc. I received a reply from a Mr. Saint Cicero with a few days.

Saint is one of those people to whom one is immediately attracted from the outset, and although I wasn't to meet him personally for some months yet (it was now the first week in April), his friendly interest and personal concern came through clearly by mail.

We corresponded almost constantly during the next two months. I held off on expressing my own opinions until I was sure I was getting advice from Saint that was clearly unbiased as a result of my views. He came through loud and clear from the beginning and the first decision we reached had to do with a mainsail design I had never heard of. Saint called it a "Satori" main, or a main with a "Satori" reef. I ordered one.

The name of the sail interested me and, later, I did a little research on the derivation of the word. I learned that in Japanese it meant "enlightenment". I conveyed this knowledge to Saint and asked him how the name happened to be selected. He responded that his partner had selected it. To the best of his knowledge, he said it had something to do with "Yoga". He agreed that "enlightenment" was about perfect and that from now on that would be what it meant.

I have never regretted my decision to select the "Satori" main. I have sold a number of them to my friends since.

Basically, it is a simple method of shortening sail in a blow, but its design also offers a means of changing the shape of a sail to provide a flat cut for beating to windward or a full cut for reaching and running. The change is made quickly and easily.

As other decisions were reached concerning her sail complement, Anuenue's wardrobe grew. We decided on two 150% genoa's, one five-ounce for light weather work and one eight-ounce for a blow. We ordered a three and a half-ounce, high-clewed reacher for the first days after Catalina while the wind would be on the beam, and a mule for rough going whenever it came. We would have a staysail to do double duty. It would fly inside the reacher when the wind was from abeam, and under the spinnaker when the wind moved aft. Finally, after much soul searching and budget stretching, we ordered three spinnakers—a three-quarter ounce for light air, a one-point-five for moderate air, and a "bullet-proof" two-point-two storm chute. The spinnakers were to be white top and bottom, with the colors of the rainbow running from leach to leach across the high full breast. Anuenue was a demanding woman. She would be well-dressed.

Before settling on this wardrobe, we had yet another decision of some magnitude to make. The other two Island N/41 owners had decided to carry a spinnaker pole two feet longer than the boat's "J" measurement called for. This would give them extra sail area in their spinnakers and head sails but would give them extra penalty in their handicaps as well. Our original policy had been, "provide for anything that would add to the GO and forget the handicap". We consequently decided first to take the long pole, but after more careful consideration and some persuasion by Dick Lindsey and Saint Cicero, we decided finally to go with a standard rig. We had arranged earlier to have ten percent of the lead ballast removed from the eight thousand pound keel to improve our surfing ability on the way down the trade winds. It was agreed by the builder and the sail maker that the lady didn't need, and in fact might object to, the extra push. I was satisfied with the final decision. I didn't want an overly tender consort on this trip. I would rather "Squeeze" for wind and more wind and hope that my Island competitors would become overpowered while I sailed relentlessly on to victory.

• • •

The question of crew was pretty well settled from the beginning. Vernon's major interest in the race was to offer this experience to his two boys, Kevin and Craig. Both boys had sailed with me on a number of Island races. Kevin was nineteen and a freshman at the University of Colorado studying engineering. He was a muscular youngster of about two hundred and twenty pounds and he had a natural feel for the helm. We had come to refer to him as our number two winch when the boys had crewed for me while racing my previous boat, the Thunderbird *Geisha*. I had number one sheet winches to handle the head sails, and once when I had been in a great hurry to get the genoa sheet in, I called to Kevin in agitated tones, "Get it in, get it in." He ignored the winch handle, grabbed the sheet and almost pulled the forestay out of the chain plate. He could handle a load. Kevin was an easy-going level-headed youngster and I was sure he would make a good crew member.

Craig was younger, only sixteen at the start of the race. He was an active high school athlete doing well in both football and wrestling. Being younger and deeply involved in these and many other high school activities, he was probably less aware of, and ready to cope with, the demands of a Transpac crewman. He was strong and agile, however, and had sailed well with me during the past year. We kidded him constantly those last few months before the race by reminding him that as the lightest member of the crew, he would no doubt be spending most of his time at the top of the mast making daily inspections and repairs to rigging aloft. I'm sure this inspired him to eat even more than he was normally capable of eating during these months in his effort to rid himself of this unenviable distinction.

Vernon had just reached the half-century mark; he was six years my junior. He had been a fighter pilot in the Pacific during the Second World War and had been sailing small boats off the beaches of Northern Oahu since. Vernon's only "big" boat time had been with me in the Newport 30 during the past year, but he had picked it up fast with a good feel of the sea. He would be ready to take the responsibilities he would have to bear as a watch captain.

My son-in-law, Jorge Rivera, had been my foredeck captain since I had pressed him into *Geisha's* service on a memorable day some four years earlier. Jorge had just returned to Hawaii from a mainland college two days before. He had never been aboard a sailboat of any kind. This particular morning, my regular crew failed to show on time for the race, so I ordered my wife and Jorge aboard. The wind was really up and the seas along with it. We were doing well, beating up to Diamond Head and then up the channel toward Koko Head. My wife, Daryl, was casting off the sheets as I short tacked, and Jorge was winching in on the other side. Then "ping" —a sail snap let go, and "ping-ping" another and another. I handed the helm over to Daryl and went forward to take down the jib which I had been carrying. Not being one to DNF (did not finish) if I could help it, I got out the genoa, my only remaining head sail, and ran it up. Geisha was so overpowered in the wind, that even reefed down, Cal 20's were catching us by now. When the sail snaps began to go on the genny, I gave it all up as a bad job and turned back. Jorge, his hands now raw from winch work, accepted a canned drink in relief, drank it and then leaned over the side and deposited drink, breakfast and, from his efforts, I'm sure, dinner from the night before, into the sea. He was to become seasick on a couple of other occasions in the future, but he never let it interfere with his sailing duties. He was regular crew from that time on.

Gordon Jay, "Gordo", had been a crew member for some months before I shanghaied Jorge. He had also served with me regularly since and was a competent hand in the cockpit. He backed up Jorge on the fore deck when required. Gordo was also eating well these last few months because, next to Craig, he was the lightest man on board and didn't want the weight relationship reversed. He was not too fond of high places in rough seas, he maintained. Gordo is a quiet bachelor of some twenty-eight or nine years. He had little to say most of the time, but, with a good sense of humor, his dry wit brought its share of chuckles from his associates. He was always ready and willing to help with whatever needed doing, from folding sails to diving over the side to scrub the bottom. He would be a good shipmate to have aboard.

With me, this made six. We still needed a seventh, and he must be, among other things, a competent navigator. The rules required an experienced navigator.

We—Vernon and I— have a "cousin-in-law" who is a Coast Guard commander with lots of sea duty in his background including racing a Coast Guard training vessel on the east coast. He, Charles Blaha, had been badly wounded while on duty in Vietnam and was at this time in a hospital in California undergoing a series of operations. It was our hope that he would complete his recovery to the point of being able to navigate for us during the race before being re-assigned to regular duty. Vernon wrote, proposing that he join us and got the letter off by mid-April.

In the meantime, we sent our entry application in to Transpac headquarters naming Charles as our navigator. We were, in time, duly accepted —provided: one, our CCA rating was submitted by June 5th; two, we submitted five glossy photographs of Anuenue before the same date; three, we submit our radio call letters as soon as possible; four, we pass a safety inspection to the satisfaction of the members of the race committee by June 20th, etc., etc., etc. We were almost in, just a few more minor details had to be completed.

As the weeks passed, I became somewhat concerned about the question of our navigator's recovery. I had studied navigation some twenty years earlier and understood it in principle. I had not, however, used a sextant at sea in practice, nor had I worked with the almanac and sight reduction table in many years. I phoned a friend, Louis Valier, who taught the subject and found he would be happy to arrange a brush-up session for me and members of my crew who were interested. We worked at it twice a week for the next five weeks by which time I was confident I could find Diamond Head with no great difficulty. Vernon, Jorge and Gordo also completed most of the study and, with some practice, would be able to shoot and reduce sights to a position line if need be.

As April passed and May began to turn into June with no definitive word from Charles, I began to scout around for a replacement. I felt by this time I had to have someone with command experience as a first pre-requisite. Competence as a navigator would be helpful, but no longer essential. We were already accepted by the Transpac Race Committee, and I felt confident this would not be changed, despite a change in crew.

I didn't have far to look. Another Hawaiian boat, which had applied and had been accepted by the race committee, withdrew in mid-May. I had sailed with one of her crewmen, Joe Dolan, on a number of occasions and knew him to be an excellent, competitive skipper. He owned a 30-foot sloop, was a good team man and also a graduate of Louis Valier's navigation class. Joe had other attributes that were to become apparent to our great good fortune later.

A final check with Charles indicated that his chances of joining us were a very long shot indeed. With regret he withdrew and wished us well. I named Joe navigator, watch captain, and second in command. Our crew was complete.

CHAPTER II

The Race circular, a document of some seven pages in fine print, arrived in due time, and the job of checking off the accomplishment of required details began in earnest. According to the circular, we would need: a self-inflating life raft with a canopy. It must be large enough to remove the entire crew and be provisioned with food and water as well as a fish line and six fish hooks. We must have two horseshoe life rings suitably mounted near the helmsman and properly attached by specific lengths of line to a "man overboard" pole with "O" flag -- such flag to meet specific design characteristics; a drawing was included with arrangement and dimensions; also attached to the life ring there must be a floating, flashing light of a certain intensity, a whistle, a package of dye marker and a drogue. We were to have aboard a suitable life preserver for each crew member, two suitable anchors (where we were to use them on the run home I wasn't sure), a two-way radio with four required channels, two compasses, two sextants, and necessary navigating charts and tables, necessary spare parts for jury-rigging in case of loss of mast, or rudder, and on, and on, and on. This, of course, was list number one.

I called a meeting of the crew at my home one evening and we prepared a first draft of list #2, all of the many things we felt should be aboard, from extra winch parts to wool socks. Our list was six pages long in double-spaced type when finally completed after a third meeting some weeks later. It had space for assignment of responsibility to the crewman selected for accomplishment of each particular detail. Jorge, for example, being an ex-Navy corpsman, was assigned to be "ship's medicine man" and would see to the stocking of a First Aid Kit. Gordo, who had done some professional photography, would procure a film supply and see that suitable photographic records were kept. Vernon would be in California early with his family, and he would shop for utensils, spare parts, and would prepare the 30-day menu required by the race committee. He would also look for any other needed supplies not available in Honolulu, supervise the commissioning of Anuenue and participate, with his boys, in shake-down cruises which were to be conducted by the factory with the assistance of the sail maker.

List #2 was run off with seven copies, and we each went to work.

• • •

The last week of May came and Vernon departed for California with plans for stepping aboard our beautifully appointed Anuenue, which had been launched a few days earlier. He and his boys were anticipating boarding a yacht all ready to go; but alas, of such fantasies are bad dreams made.

When I first heard from him a week later, he had seen Anuenue and she was a beauty, but he had not as yet been able to join in trials because the factory carpenters were still hard at work on interior joiner detail. They would be finished soon, he hoped, and he would then send me a report on performance.

Another week passed and another letter arrived. Anuenue had been to sea, skippered by a friend of Dick Lindsey, and had done well, winning her class in a race to Catalina and back. Vernon and the boys had not made the trip, however, since the race had come on a weekend they spent in San Francisco. Anuenue was now back in her borrowed slip and unable to go to sea again. It seems she had raced to Catalina with a borrowed main boom. Hers was not as yet modified to handle the Satori main sail she carried. There were also a number of other minor matters to attend to. Her radio was not yet installed. Her spreader lights were shorted out. She did not, as yet, have a boot around her mast, and she consequently took water there whenever it came aboard. Her cabin top vents were not as yet installed. Her knot meter and log had not yet arrived. She had no suitable topping lift for her main boom.

Vernon suggested that it might be wise for me to move my departure from Honolulu forward a few days, in fact, immediately, in the hope that my presence could be used to apply more pressure. He wanted thus to assure early completion of these and other details needing immediate attention so that we would have adequate shake-down time. I took Vernon's plea for assistance as nothing more than a sign of nerves before the big event and went merrily about my business, working out the details I had assigned to myself. I was certain that his next letter would report all was well and ready, but it was just not meant to be.

His next letter arrived two days before my scheduled departure on June 20, the date we were to be ready for inspection. It listed newly found shortcomings in our beautiful ship, continued lack of progress, and ended with a plea for my immediate departure. It was time for me to become concerned; Anuenue had the inspection to stand day after tomorrow. I got a note off to Vernon, consulted hurriedly with the other crew members about remaining details at home, and left on the evening of the 18th for Los Angeles.

The trip up was smooth and uneventful. With my new found attention to navigating details, however, I did take interest in watching the North Star climb from its resting place at 21 degrees above the horizon over Hawaii to its perch at 34 degrees as we approached Los Angeles. It took only five hours to climb to this height on the airplane up to the Coast. I would spend some twelve to thirteen days bringing it back down to where it belonged after July 4th.

I was met in the Los Angeles airport by Jimmy Dugan, a gentleman, a scholar and a marine hardware dealer from the Newport area. Jimmy would prove to be a strong local pillar for me to lean on in moments of need during the two weeks ahead before the race. He dropped me off at the Newport address Vernon had given me and I rapped on the door to awaken Kevin and Craig. My note to Vernon had not yet arrived and Vernon had driven to San Francisco the evening before with Anne, his wife, and his younger daughter, who were flying East to visit Anne's family.

The boys took me in, and Kevin started preparing breakfast. He called my attention to what he was doing. He emptied a few ounces of ingredients from a small plastic bag into a pan and added water. The concoction became scrambled eggs and ham after it cooked a while and was downright palatable.

They had been experimenting with lightweight dehydrated foods in preparation for the race. The breakfast was good and came complete with a reconstituted jelly. They showed me cellophane packages of beef stew, stroganoff, chicken curry, vegetables of all kinds, fruit cocktail and even dehydrated peanut butter. I was impressed. They had indeed been making progress, even though Anuenue still sat unfinished at her slip.

After I had eaten and changed to working togs, Kevin drove me to the mooring. My first view showed even another unfinished detail. Her transom was to carry a rainbow with her name and port laid across it in gold. The rainbow had been sprayed in, but the lettering was only blacked in. She looked somewhat undressed with her underwear exposed. Her lines were strong and sharp, however, and she looked to be the thoroughbred we hoped she was.

I spent all morning and a good part of the afternoon crawling in and about her making notes of the shortcomings I found that should be brought to the builders' attention. I also listed other jobs that would need the attention of her crew before final departure. In the afternoon Kevin drove me to Lindsey Plastics where I met Dick and discussed with him our plans and problems. I liked Dick from the start. He is personable and soft-spoken, and he assured me we would be ready on time.

I broached with Dick the subject of planning an emergency steering system in case of rudder failure. Transpac rules required that I be ready at safety inspection to show how I would cope with this eventuality, should it arise.

Dick was firm in his opinion concerning the usual emergency device, a sweep on the end of a spinnaker pole. He felt such a device would probably get me by the safety committee but, in his judgment, we would be in no position to continue racing with such an arrangement. We agreed I would want to continue racing if possible.

Dick suggested that a long hardwood 2 X 12 plank be fashioned into a rudder and hardware be procured for quick attachment to the transom. We could attach the emergency tiller, already provided, to this. We sketched a rough plan; he offered the use of his shop and said he would call the designers of Anuenue to get their thoughts on the problem.

I was introduced to the plant superintendent, Mack McCutchen. Mack would order in a plank and have tools and a work space ready for me tomorrow afternoon at 5:30. I wanted to do the job myself. Having previously built two boats, I was reasonably skilled in wood work and would enjoy the activity.

The work was accomplished as planned. The designer's drawings, when they arrived, showed a rudder almost identical to the one I had fashioned in rough form. His was a foot shorter, so I cut off the plank to match, and finished smoothing it into an airfoil cross-section and delivered it to Anuenue where it was stowed beneath the cockpit deck.

As I had left home for Los Angeles, my wife's last words had been, "Remember the broken tiller fittings. Go over the steering with a microscope."

Solving this problem to my satisfaction took a big load off my mind. Of the previous four boats I have owned and sailed, three had lost steering control while underway. Two of them had done so while racing on a downwind leg with a spinnaker flying. I was not without respect for this problem.

I arranged to be at the boat the following morning to meet the Lindsey work crew and left for the apartment to complete, at Dick's suggestion, a list of every possible thing that needed attention.

Vernon returned that evening and we went through my list of incomplete details aboard Anuenue and compared it with his list. We combined the two and had a page and a half of notes.

We then examined his copy of list number two along with mine and brought them up to date, indicating items completed, and adding new items that had come to our attention.

Next we opened and re-examined the race circular noting and checking off items completed, and taking special note of important goods to be procured or important jobs to be accomplished. Vernon then went over a list of food and sundries he had prepared for my examination and, finally, we made up from all of this a "tomorrow" list, which included finding out if we could get a postponement of our safety inspection.

We then went to bed. I was running short on sleep as a result of my flight up, but this was a condition I was to become accustom to until my return home.

The next morning we dropped the two boys off at the boat to await the arrival of the men from the factory, and we headed out to work down the list of chores we had set for ourselves for the day. We arranged for a postponement of our safety inspection to the following week. We called on the sailmaker and found he was almost finished with our 2.2 ounce spinnaker. We ordered from him a sail repair kit and "tie-down" cover for our inflatable life raft which would be carried on the cabin top. We stopped by the radio shop to hurry along the installation and tuning of our radio, and we called on the instrument man to schedule the "swinging" of our compass.

When we noticed the time, we knew the boys would be starving as it was well past noon. So we picked up sandwiches and returned to the boat to see how things were progressing. The workmen had not arrived. Finally, during our lunch, one man appeared from the factory. He came, he said, to fix the door to the head that was not closing properly, and knew nothing of spreader lights, cabin vents, knot meters, etc. And so started the frustrating last two weeks before the race.

Vernon and I shopped the afternoon through, concentrating on items we needed aboard for our inspection, and returned with them to Anuenue where they were to be installed or stored. The boys kept busy working down the list we had prepared for them, doing the installing and storing.

I kept my 5:30 date at the plant to start work on the emergency rudder. I reminded Dick and Mack that their workmen had failed to show at the slip, accepted their apologies and assurance that tomorrow would be different, and then I went about my work.

The second day went almost like the first, and the third day almost like the second. We would shop the day away trying to locate needed items, stopping periodically to prod the factory, the radio shop or the instrument man. We would work aboard until 8 or 9 pm. each evening and then return home for dinner and another run through over lists, preparing a new list of the "neediest" needs for tomorrow. We gradually wore down the list of items needed for the safety inspection. The radio man really did exist; he got our set installed and tuned. And the sun, in sunny California, finally did come through long enough for the instrument man to swing the compass. We were ready for inspection on Thursday, a week after I arrived.

We passed inspection with no difficulty and set about preparing new lists. The rest of the crew, Joe,

Jorge, and Gordo would arrive tomorrow morning, so work was apportioned for them to do.

There were races scheduled for Saturday and Sunday out of Los Angeles as "warm up" for the Transpac fleet, and new lists would have to reflect the needs for these events.

We had engaged in no shake-down. We had sailed Anuenue around Newport harbor a few times in gentle breezes, but, on the two occasions we had ventured out, the wind had dropped off to nothing, and we had sailed back in to find the breeze still blowing in and around the harbor.

Our plans had called for at least one overnight trip out beyond Catalina, where we could find some wind with a bit of force to it and some lumpy seas so we could learn how Anuenue would behave when the going got rough. It was beginning to look as though the shakedown would be nothing more than a gentle tremor provided by the flat water and gentle breezes off Southern California. The list of things yet to be accomplished was too long to allow for anymore. We didn't realize how regrettable this circumstance was to become.

Joe, Jorge, and Gordo arrived on schedule the following morning. After a hasty breakfast, Vernon dropped the rest of us off at the slip while he went out around the town to work down the list for the day, mainly buying supplies for the weekend in Los Angeles and paying bills for various services.

The three newly arrived crew members crawled around Anuenue for a while, poking, patting, opening and peeking until familiarity set in. They then got to work on my morning's list of things to do aboard. By noon, Joe had finished making a spinnaker net and had inspected all rigging aloft. Jorge had his medical supplies and other gear stowed and Gordo had a good start on his photo album materials.

Vernon returned at noon with food and drink and, after doing justice to these, we slipped our lines, backed out into the stream, hoisted sail and were under way for the first time as a complete team. The boys were excited and happy; Anuenue performed for them beautifully. She would tack through a mere eighty degrees when hard on the wind and the breeze that afternoon was good to us. The company we kept was interesting also. As we had backed out of our slip, the big Canadian ketch *Mir* had gone by under power. A few moments later, after rounding Balboa Island, we tacked right under the transom of *Windward Passage* moored at her slip. Both of these big beauties would be contenders for first to finish honors in the Transpac. We turned at the end of the harbor, reached down the channel and out to the sea. After, a few moments, the wind died to a zephyr so we came about and joined the traffic back. Each of the newly arrived crew members took a turn at the wheel when we got back into the harbor, and you could see the "Hornblower" in their eyes as they felt the power and response of Anuenue when she heeled and surged with the touch of breeze in her sails.

As darkness approached, we returned to our mooring and home to the apartment. The crew needed sleep. We were scheduled to meet the other two N-41's off the Balboa Yacht Club the following morning at 6:30. From there Fred Smales, skippering John Moore's *Americana*, would lead us up the coast some fifteen miles to the Los Angeles Yacht Club in the Los Angeles harbor, where we would enter the shake down races and be off to Point Fermin for the noon start. We would have to leave early as we would need to gas up before the 6:30 rendezvous.

Vernon planned to take the rest of us to the slip in the morning and then drive to Los Angeles. We wanted the car while there over the weekend. We set the alarm for 5 a.m. and all hit the sack early. We were quite a gang sprawled out in a two bedroom apartment, but with spare cushions from the furniture, we made it and were soon asleep on the eve of our first real trials.

With some effort and much nagging, we got everyone up and ready in the morning, met *Americana* and *Hawaiiana* as scheduled, and were off to Los Angeles. After clearing the harbor, Kevin volunteered to cook our first breakfast at sea, and we could soon detect the aroma of ham and eggs floating up from the galley. The aroma was followed by Kevin with a distressed look on his face and a plaintive note in his voice; he said, "We have no salt and pepper."

Lists, lists, and more lists, and still not one included salt and pepper.

Hawaiiana and *Americana* each carried a cook aboard and as *Hawaiiana* was nearby, I hailed her to join me alongside and requested assistance in this most important matter. Jay Moore laughed heartily and called back, "We have nothing but sweet rolls aboard." "Some cook they have," I thought. *Americana* was too far ahead to overtake so we ate our tasteless breakfast in silence as we powered along on our way to Los Angeles. I did take time to start another list, however — one headed with "Salt and Pepper."

CHAPTER III

The coast of California was a hazy shadow off to starboard, disappearing sometimes completely in the ever-present smog of Los Angeles. I sent Joe below to work a compass course to the entrance in the Los Angeles breakwater just in case I became separated from the other boats on the way up. Joe returned with the course 285 degrees magnetic. We were holding just outside of this at 280 degrees, I assumed for some good reason, so I continued to follow *Americana*, now a quarter of a mile ahead. Soon a large object still hazy in the smog loomed ahead off the starboard bow. As we drew closer, we finally identified it as an oil well structure, big, bleak and black, standing alone, pecking constantly at the ocean floor as it brought up fuel to feed the fires to create the smog in which to hide itself. A giant, multi-legged industrial ostrich, I thought. We soon passed it, leaving it to the starboard, and before it disappeared from sight astern, another—its mate, I presumed, appeared ahead. We soon left it also astern, turned slightly to starboard in pursuit of our convoy leader, and there off to the right was the long low breakwater of the outer Los Angeles harbor. We followed them through the entrance and on into the depths of the harbor, identifying and checking off landmarks as they slowly moved toward us from out of the murk.

Americana suddenly disappeared, swallowed up by the Los Angeles background. She was followed by *Hawaiiana*. We headed for the spot, found an inner breakwater with a small opening and entered cautiously with some trepidation. There to our right was the fleet. We were invited by those ashore to a mooring alongside a floating pier, idled in and tied up. We were at the Los Angeles Yacht Club. It was 10 a.m. the first shake down race would start at noon off Point Fermin.

I dispatched Craig to locate his father and headed for the club office to fulfill the entry requirements. The club officer I found informed me that the committee boat had already left for the starting line and that I would have to go alongside when I got out to pick up race instructions. I had been properly entered by telephone from Newport, he said. I asked him how long it would take me to get to the starting line, and he answered I should allow one hour and fifteen minutes to be safe. I returned to the pier expecting to find Vernon and the others awaiting my information and instructions. Craig had returned from his scouting trip of the club's waterfront with no news. Vernon had not yet arrived.

It was now 10:30 a.m. I dispatched Craig again this time to the club office to ascertain if any message had been left for us. He returned in a few moments with the word that there were no messages.

It was 10:40 a.m. I sent Craig up to the parking lot and asked him to wait and watch for five minutes and then, if his father had not arrived, to return.

Americnan, *Hawaiiana* and most other boats in the race were casting off their lines and leaving.

My starting time was actually 12:10 as my rating of 34.9 placed me in "C" as the California yachtsmen divided into classes. *Americnan* at 36.0 and *Hawaiiana* at 36.2 were in Class "B" and would start at 12:05. The big Class "A" boats would start at noon. I could still wait a few minutes.

Craig returned at 10:45 with no news of his father.

I must confess, I was concerned. The few trips I had made on California freeways were enough to convince me that the trip we planned to Hawaii was as safe as sleeping on a couch in one's own living room when compared with the 15 mile trip from Newport to Los Angeles by freeway.

At 10:55, I ordered the engine started and all lines cast off and taken aboard. If there is one important rule in racing, it is the first rule, "Be at the starting line early." We would have to hurry to check in with the committee boat and pick up our instructions. We would have little or no time to check wind and current conditions and none to time the length of a run down the line.

A light breeze had sprung up so I ordered main and 5-ounce genoa hoisted, and we motor-sailed at our best available speed toward the buoy off Point Fermin.

Anuenue was either particularly fast, or the LAYC officer was particularly conservative. We arrived at the committee boat, not far from the buoy and picked up our instructions at 11:50.

I could have waited another ten minutes, and as it turned out, this would have been enough. We were to learn later that Vernon arrived, working his way through the maze of South Los Angeles, just after we cleared the inner breakwater and headed out.

• • •

In Hawaii, we never, never experience fog, so it was with some measure of interest that the mooing like that of a cow we heard, increasing in decibels, as we approached the buoy off Point Fermin was, in fact, the fog horn lowing constantly to warn the seamen that a treacherous rocky headland was nearby.

We "ran the line" once and cleared the buoy just before Class "A" started in 5 to 8 knot breezes from the northwest. We reached on up the coast for 2 and 1/2 minutes and were back just short of the starting area as Class "B" started. Jorge was holding the stopwatch. He started it as the Class "B" signal was hoisted, and we reached on up the line toward the committee boat. Jorge counted down. With two minutes remaining, we were just short of the end of the line. I called, "jibe ho," and we went over following the rest of Class "C" diagonally away from the line. This is the big league, I thought. I don't want to be early and have to come around again. I held the run away until there was just one minute left, ordered "ready about"—"helm's a'lee" and we came about and headed for our start. As the signal went down signifying 30 seconds to go, Joe called, "Come on, come on—there's all the room in the world."

I'd been too cautious. We got across on the outer end with clear air, but we were back with the middle of the fleet—no place for champions. I'd be bolder next time.

As we cleared the line and began to move in earnest, a call from the foredeck warned me we were closing in fast on a big K-50 which was dead ahead about 50 feet away. I pointed up a bit ordering sheets hardened to the limit to go above her when Joe called, "Hold it. The Santana ahead of the K-50 is beginning to luff her. If we time it right, we can get through to the leeward."

I called back to let me know when. I couldn't see either boat under the genoa. I cautioned the rest of the crew to be ready to ease sheets just as Joe called, "Now." We eased sheets slightly. I fell down until I could see both the other boats, and Anuenue surged forward.

She is a lovely lady. In seconds, we were abeam, to leeward and in a few more seconds, after hardening sheets again, we were dead ahead and well clear of the fracas going on behind us.

Joe went below to check our heading against the race course to Catalina and we settled down for the long beat to windward.

We were "in action". It was a good feeling.

Thirty minutes after the start, we had worked up through and to weather of the "C" fleet. We spotted only one more boat, a popular forty-footer still to weather of us by about three hundred yards and abeam. He must have tacked earlier and gone up the California shore before coming over to starboard and heading for Catalina. We used him for a reference point and set about "fine trimming" Anuenue. Within another half hour we had crossed ahead of the forty-footer and were leaving him behind off our leeward quarter. Anuenue could really climb upwind.

Catalina slowly took form out of the murk. We could see many Class "A" and "B" boats off to port and ahead. I ordered the field glasses out for an appraisal of the wind conditions they were encountering and discovered that those further ahead were in light and variable air. Where we were, we still had ten to twelve knots of wind and holding steady.

Before leaving Honolulu, we had a number of meetings with the crews from the Hawaiian boats. Fred Smales, a gentleman and sportsman of first quality, who was now skippering *Americana* had been more than generous with his "local knowledge" of this area. Fred had sailed many years in Southern California waters and was well schooled for the trip to Catalina and back. He had also participated in a number of Transpac races, and was a great help to us neophytes in preparing for the event.

Fred's advice concerning this trip to Catalina had included the warning: "Never tack out in the channel."

He told us the currents would be against us there, and that we should run in close to Catalina, above Arrow Point, where we could find fair winds spilling out of the valleys that would carry us up to the west end.

We were still well out in the channel when we spotted the boats up ahead and to leeward running out of air. My inclination was to tack and avoid the dead spot if I could. I held on for a few moments, however, and asked Jorge, who had the glasses, to check the rest of the fleet and see what they were up to. Jorge called, "Look, isn't that a '41 coming up toward us?"

I took the glasses, as Joe now had the helm, and adjusted them to the white sloop on port tack about a quarter of a mile away off our port bow.

"It's Fred!" I cried.

Our spirits were boundless. *Americana* had started five minutes ahead of us and now here she was coming up to our track and clearly further from the mark than we.

My inclination to tack regardless of Fred's advice had been correct, I concluded. He had obviously done so to avoid the "flat" spots ahead.

I crossed his bow about a hundred yards ahead of him, went on until I was directly to windward and came about to parallel his course. Fred tacked again and I followed, keeping directly to windward between him and the mark.

One of the crew from the foredeck called to me that the first boat, as yet unidentified, had rounded the flag up near the west end of Catalina and was heading back. I looked forward and saw her "chute" fill. I called back to watch for the next one to round and to try to pick up the flag. Joe was still at the helm, and we continued to cover Fred and the Columbia 50 that was booming along in his wake by now, having tacked up from leeward.

We counted five Class “A” boats up between us and the mark. The boys had now picked out the flag as the second one rounded and started back.

We were about a half a mile away. Fred apparently spotted the flag also and he went back over onto a port tack. We followed to cover him and were now beating northwest parallel to the shoreline of Catalina.

I ordered the three quarter ounce chute brought up from below and all made ready to go up after we rounded the flag which was slowly drawing abeam. The other three big “A” boats were around and coming back toward us, their big spinnakers splashing bright swatches of color across the drab Catalina background.

I didn’t wait for Fred to tack this time. As the flag neared a position a little ahead of our beam, I ordered us about to starboard and we started in. A check ahead indicated we were barely making the mark. I cautioned Joe to hold her up as best he could without killing speed. It appeared as though the breeze should bend enough around the end of Catalina to lift us as we drew closer. If it didn’t, we would have to tack again to get around. We were to leave the mark to port, according to race instructions.

I looked back. Fred, with the Columbia 50 close astern and to leeward, had crossed my stern and was going on before coming about. He had apparently checked my track as he crossed and saw that Anuenue was having to "pinch" to make the mark. He came about a hundred or so yards above me and started in.

At about three hundred yards out, "Lady Luck" gave us a friendly kiss on the cheek. She was just luring us into her trap in order to make the "slap" she would give us sting more when she administered it. The wind bent as I had hoped and we would make the mark easily.

I replaced Joe at the helm as he went forward with Jorge and Craig to supervise the setting of the chute. Gordo would "tend" the sheet and Kevin would haul in on the after guy. We were ready.

Two small outboard runabouts joined us as we approached, buzzing about like bees, camera shutters clicking. They would jump as though they were stung soon.

The flag was a hundred feet away as I ordered, "prepare to jibe," followed by "jibe ho!" As the mark came under my lee bow I pulled hard on the helm. We were well into our turn around the flag, the main boom almost ready to go across, when the wheel spun free in my hands and fell back against the side of the cockpit.

"We're out of control," I called, as Anuenue spun back to windward and the runabouts scattered.

I must have sounded a bit plaintive. The crew kidded me about the tone of my voice for some time after it was all over, but at the moment they jumped to like veterans.

Our head had swung through the wind; Joe had let all sheets go, and we were back on a port tack bobbing slowly away from the mark, fluttering like a wounded bird.

I ordered a quick examination of the steering mechanism below the cockpit. Joe popped back out and reported all in good order there.

I ordered the emergency tiller and tools out so that we could remove the teak plate hiding the head of the rudder shaft and bolt on the tiller. Craig dumped the whole kit of tools on the cockpit floor, and Gordo dived under the cockpit deck with a knife to cut loose the tiller that we had lashed there out of the way.

In not over two minutes the tiller was attached, and I was hauling on it, urging the crew to bring sheets in fast, fast, fast, so we could get about and back to the mark. We had drifted about a hundred yards away from it. As I looked back, *Americana* had rounded and was settling her chute. The Columbia 50 was just rounding into her jibe. We had lost them. We would have to "hump" to get them back. There was no one else close.

We got around and had our chute flying in short order. Anuenue was a bear to handle with the tiller, but she could be handled —in these light breezes.

Joe went below to plot a course back to Los Angeles Harbor. His plot indicated a course slightly below *Americana* and the Columbia 50. I aligned Anuenue on the heading, and we settled back for a careful examination of our steering system. The tools were still on the cockpit deck, so Joe picked up a wrench and removed the nut that held the wheel hub in place.

I have censored his remarks as the wheel came off. I assure you they were colorful. There was no key in the keyway. The wheel had been held in place by the friction of the nut only. We were fortunate to have discovered it now rather than a week or so later. I realized that this is what "shake-downs" are for. Joe's mechanical know-how and ingenuity began to make itself evident. He went below and within a few moments was back with an end broken off the handle of a file. He fitted it into the keyway and replaced the wheel.

It was working, and although something was rubbing and binding a bit somewhere, Anuenue was easier to handle with the wheel than with the tiller.

We disassembled the tiller, cleaned up the tools, put them away, and looked around for our competition.

We all hesitated to voice what appeared self-evident. We feared, I'm sure, it was just wishful thinking but, we were ever so slowly over-taking *Americana* and the Columbia 50 that had now passed her. We had presumed that, with her larger spinnaker, *Americana* would leave us behind in the run back to Los Angeles. Fred continued to hold a course slightly above the buoy off Los Angeles harbor. That would be our next mark. Joe double checked the compass course and we determined to hold as we were. Slowly we crept up and continued to diverge slightly from the course Fred was sailing. I began to wonder if his local knowledge held some secret that I didn't know about conditions ahead. I voiced my concern, and we discussed it for a while. At this point, in about mid-channel, we had come abeam of him and watched with admiration as his crew doused one spinnaker and had another flying in less than thirty seconds. It was beautiful crew work, but we continued to pull ahead slowly. We decided that if we wanted to be the first Hawaiian boat in, we would have to cover Fred, so I altered my course a few degrees to parallel his.

In another hour we picked up the first "A" boat rounding the buoy and heading for the harbor entrance. We were between Fred and the buoy and two hundred yards ahead. The Columbia 50 was two hundred feet ahead and to windward of us. We wouldn't catch her unless we were lucky. We weren't. She rounded a safe two hundred feet ahead of us, didn't foul anything as her chute came down, and started her short reach to the finish line just inside the harbor. We followed, also without "foul-up", and finished elated.

It was a little difficult to keep our chests from puffing out excessively as we tied up in the harbor in the presence of family and friends of our competitors who were awaiting their arrival.

We finished first in Class and second overall. A smaller boat, not eligible for Transpac, had saved her time on us to take first over-all honors. Oh! but for that key.........!

CHAPTER IV

We were still unable to locate Vernon, and there was no message from him. Finally, Kevin suggested we call the apartment back in Newport Beach and when we did, sure enough, he answered. He had decided, after missing us in Los Angeles, that he could do more good for our cause by going back and getting to work on the remaining shopping than he could by waiting around the Yacht Club. He was elated by our victory, and as it was by now after 9 p.m., decided to sleep in Newport and drive up in the morning. This time he knew the route, and would join us in time for the Sunday shake down race.

Back at the boat, I found Joe in misery. His eyes were sun-burned and swollen, causing him a considerable measure of pain. In Hawaii, most of our racing is in bright sunshine. We consequently habitually protect ourselves from it with suitable hats and glasses. With the cooler weather and the solid overcast that had prevailed throughout the day, Joe had neglected wearing his dark glasses and his hat, and he was now paying the price.

Jorge gave him relief as best he could, with the medical supplies we had, before we bedded down for the night, but in the morning his eyes were an angry red, still swollen and the pain had not subsided.

When Vernon arrived we checked Joe off the crew roster and sent him back in the car to get medical attention. He assured us he could see well enough to drive.

• • •

As far as Yacht racing annals are concerned, the Sunday race up to a spar buoy off Marineland and back doesn't exist. The spar had drifted away, leaving no turning mark at the windward end of the course. As a result, the race was abandoned.

I did get off with a bolder start, right on the flag, and led the "C" fleet out of the harbor. The start was a mile or so inside the outer breakwater.

I spent most of the beat to weather experimenting to see just how close to the wind I could hold Anuenue and still keep her moving. I learned she could be pinched up very high if need be, but that she paid for it in speed. I also practiced techniques for keeping her moving as we came about. We learned a lot that we would need to know before heading for home.

We raced the course to the vicinity of the missing mark, turned with the rest of the fleet, and sailed back. We came in across the finish line in the outer harbor and jibed to head out again on a course back to Newport. We still had a mad five days ahead of us before noon July 4th, the following Friday, and had to get back to our base to get at it.

At the apartment, we found Joe feeling much better. He had found the required medical attention and would be ready for active duty tomorrow.

• • •

Monday, June 30: Anuenue still had no log; her spreader lights were still dark, the inside compartments under the main cabin bunks where we would carry stores were still not sealed from the bilges. She had no forward vent and her mast boot was not complete.

A workman did arrive Monday morning to seal up the mast where it came through the deck, and he returned later with the foredeck vent.

Vernon and I were out on the town again for still needed hardware. We finally found extra pawls and springs for our Barlow winches. We stopped by a large department store and bought white slacks for crew members to wear to the Instruction Dinner and other social affairs. We laid in a supply of dark glasses and hats to see that there wasn't a repeat of the eye problem, and we arranged with a large local boatyard to haul Anuenue so that we could get her bottom cleaned and smoothed for the race.

Aboard Anuenue, the boys got strips of carpet laced around the port side of the bow pulpit, the port spreader of the mast and the lower end of the port shrounds. We would be on starboard tack for a long time and needed to protect our sails from chafing. They completed dozens of other chores to secure fittings and protect standing and running rigging from the rigors of the race.

Late Monday afternoon, we again called Dick to inform him we would not be available Wednesday as we would be hauled out; Thursday we told him we would be packing and loading stores all day and would have to leave finally for Los Angeles Thursday evening. The boat must be finished tomorrow. Dick as he had all along, assured us we would be ready.

We made our list for Tuesday and went to bed sure we would never make it by Friday but determined to try.

• • •

<u>Tuesday, July 1:</u> We awoke early, got our breakfast out of the way and split up into teams. Vernon, with Kevin and Jorge, headed off in one car (we had borrowed a second one from a friend) to buy food supplies and get them back to the apartment. They would then begin dividing them into piles for each day of the trip according to the menu already prepared by Vernon. They were to be packaged in large plastic bags and dated. During the race then, we

would draw the package for the day from storage and place it in a convenient galley cabinet where it would be handy for preparation as the day went by.

We had planned a complete menu for two weeks. We would carry just general stores—corned beef, crackers and canned fruits and vegetables to fulfill the remainder of the 30-day Transpac requirement. Earlier I had impressed Vernon so thoroughly with the importance of cutting weight, that he had planned for only two or three days of canned food, all the rest was to be lightweight dehydrated stores in order to help us consume what we considered the excessive load of water we were required to carry. We had quite a discussion concerning the subject.

I finally convinced Vernon that we couldn't be so totally dependent on dehydrated foods. A broken mast or rudder could keep us at sea much longer than expected, and we would need both water and food to subsist over a longer period; or, a contaminated water tank would require conservation of water in other tanks and we would need food that was not dependent on water. We weren't to realize how important our decision to increase canned stores was for some ten days yet.

While Vernon and his crew went shopping for food, Joe, Gordo and I went to the boat to work down the lists of "musts" before departure.

Craig stayed at the apartment to await the arrival of his sister Terrill. Terrill is Vernon's oldest child. She was living and working in Santa Monica but had made time available to help us get ready for the race. I don't know what we'd have done without her.

Terrill and Craig were to go shopping for light blue T-shirts for the members of the crew. We had rainbow (Anuenue) emblems made before we left home and these were to be sewn on the shirts to complete our uniforms. The uniforms would be needed for a christening ceremony planned for the new Hawaiian boats this evening at the Balboa Yacht Club.

Aboard Anuenue, we found a factory man installing the log. A workman from the subcontractor who had installed the lights had been there and left, unable to find the short in the spreader lights. He had left his roll of wire behind. Joe took a look at the wire and said: "Come on, haul me up the mast." We, Gordo and I, hauled him with his tools up to the spreader and secured him in place.

In a few moments he called for a roll of light line and a heavy bolt. We sent them up on the flag halyard. A few moments later, Joe suggested someone go to the base of the mast inside the boat, peer through the hole where the wires came out of the mast and look for the bolt tied to the light line. We found it, hooked it with a wire coat hanger bent to fit the hole, and soon we had the end of the wire from the roll that was left behind tied to the line and were feeding it into the hole in the mast as Joe hauled it aloft at the spreader. Before the morning was gone, we had the old spreader light wires cut off and the new ones wired in. When we threw the switch, we had lights. Maybe we would make it after all.

We, Vernon, Joe, and I, had to break loose shortly after noon for a quick trip up to Los Angeles to attend a meeting of all skippers and navigators. At the meeting, we would receive final race instructions, learn our handicap, and what the division into classes would be. The boys were left to clean up and dress Anuenue for the christening that evening.

The results of the meeting could not have been more to our liking. When we were handed the final list of entries showing rating and class we discovered we had the lowest rating in Class “C”. Everyone else in the class would give us time. This included the other Newport’s, all Cal 40’s and several other boats. Things were really looking good. We collected our sheaf of papers, which included weather maps for recording and plotting the weather code as it was broadcast each morning, radio communication instructions, handicaps, etc.

Back at the slip we found Anuenue all decked out with signal flags up the forestay, over the masthead and down the backstay. Her decks were spotless. She was dressed in her Sunday best. The factory work had been completed except for sealing the storage compartments from the bilge. While we were pondering what we might do to protect stores in these compartments, Mack McKutchen stopped by to check us out and wish us well. We told him of the sealing problem and he said, “Don’t go away—I’ll be back in ten minutes.” He left and returned a few moments later with an armload of materials. Within thirty minutes the bilges were sealed off from the storage compartments. Mack almost asphyxiated himself in the process, but the last job was done and we would be ready.

When we returned to the apartment, we found everyone cleaning up and getting dressed in the new uniforms which had been purchased and prepared by Terrill. We fell in with the ranks and got ourselves ready for the christening.

• • •

We were quite a sight I'm sure, all dressed in our slacks, our new shirts and dark blue blazers, as we powered down the bay to the Balboa Yacht Club, all flags flying.

It would be nice to report that the christening came off without a "hang up" but such was not to be. We were getting so we expected trouble, and were seldom surprised by not finding it.

This time it came in the form of a message to the effect that the friend from the Islands, who had planned to deliver a hundred orchid leis to us for the occasion, couldn't make it down to Newport. We would have to send someone up to get them from the airline. Joe had ordered the orchids and Kevin knew how to get to the airport, so these two were appointed to complete the mission. The rest of us, including Terrill, took Anuenue down to the Yacht Club, tied her up and joined in the festivities.

In time, as the crowd gathered, all of the new Hawaiian boats -- the three N/41's and a Cal 40, were moored beam to beam. With the cameras clicking, a lady for each boat (Terrill for ours) poised herself on the foreword deck and shattered her bottle of champagne across the bow. We had waited as long as we could for the return of the boys with the leis but it was getting dark and the show had to go on.

Joe and Kevin finally arrived just as the party was about to break up, and we made a mad dash to get the leis distributed to the remaining guests. There had been a "paper" hang-up at the airport, and I guess the boys had to threaten mayhem to get the leis at all.

As we were weaving our way through the boats in the harbor back to our own borrowed slip, I heard a strange clicking emanating from the galley. On investigating, I discovered I had a right handy crew indeed. They had "liberated" a half dozen bottles of champagne from the bar at the party and stashed them in the ice box. Had I known how important that champagne was to become later, I would have spun around to take them back for another raid on the bar.

• • •

Wednesday July 2: We rolled out soon after dawn and Vernon delivered Joe, Jorge and me to the slip to take Anuenue to the yard for her 8:30 haul-out date. The rest of the crew stayed at the apartment to finish packing food and other consumer goods. We were met at the yard dock by a hail from the pier.

"Tie'er up there," and the figure on the dock pointed at the slip immediately below a huge crane.

Within a few minutes our back stay was removed, two huge straps were slung under Anuenue's belly, and the crane lifted her like a toy ship out of a bathtub and plopped her down on a cradle. We looked around and discovered we were back in "high society" again; *Windward Passage* was high and dry just a few feet from our bow.

Thus began another most frustrating day.

The yard superintendent came over and we checked Anuenue's bottom together. Her paint job appeared to have been done by amateurs. There were heavy ridges showing each brush stroke, some of them running crosswise to her hull rather than fore and aft as they should. He assigned a crew of four men to start sanding down the ridges while Joe and I busied ourselves with remaining rigging chores.

Noon came and went and a check of the four conversational characters with the sandpaper indicated they hadn't yet finished one side of the bottom. They would work like beavers when the superintendent walked by, but, after he had gone, they would start chattering again. They seemed never to move, and when they did take a swipe at the bottom with their sandpaper it was always in the same place. By 2 p.m. they had worn most of the paint off the starboard side, and when a workman started scraping the paint off the port side with a sharpened putty knife, I blew my stack and went to find the superintendent to remind him that the race we had entered started July 4th this year, not next.

He came back, read the riot act to the workmen, gave Joe and me permission to join in the work (which permission he had previously refused) and we had her bottom smooth by 3 p.m.

We waited again for another workman to come along to spray her bottom with Teflon which would give it a smooth, glassy finish. He finally came, he sprayed, we wiped down, and Anuenue was back in the water again by 5 p.m. We had expected to be finished by noon.

• • •

We had been moored until this time at a private dock on the south shore of Lido Island. Our apartment was across the bay adjacent to Newport Beach. When we returned with Anuenue, we tied up at another private pier on the beach side which was located just a block from our apartment. Vernon had arranged this through a friend so that the loading of stores would be more convenient. We hurried home after tying up, to dress for the Instruction Dinner which was planned for crews and friends of Transpac Yachts at the Biltmore Hotel in downtown Los Angeles this evening.

When we returned to the apartment, we found the floor covered with green plastic bags filled with food and dated for use. A jumble of other packages were scattered in boxes or loose on one side of the room. It appeared to be enough for an army—I didn't see how we would get it all aboard.

The Instruction Dinner was a noisy, gala affair. We just ran into one snag—we lost Vernon again, along with Kevin and Terrill. The rest of us had dressed first and departed in one car. Vernon was to follow with the other when they were ready.

At the hotel we stalled our dinner as long as we could; we searched about the hotel; we even called the state police to see if an accident had been reported involving Vernon and his children. There were no reports. There was no answer when we rang up the apartment. We became truly concerned. The dinner with its accompaniment of speeches lasted well into the night. When it was over, we went back to the telephone in the hotel and called the police again. There was still no report. We called the apartment again and Vernon answered. They had started for L. A. soon after we had, but had been misdirected a number of times, seeking the route to the hotel, and had ended up touring most of greater Los Angeles in search of the party. When 9 o'clock rolled by and they still hadn't found the hotel, they returned to Newport where they dined out before going back to the apartment.

Vernon had studied navigation with me, and had practiced diligently, but I concluded after this experience that I should keep him occupied with other duties during the race home.

• • •

Thursday, July 3: Our schedule for the last day before the race read as follows:

1. Get the stores aboard and stowed.
2. Fill the water tanks and spare containers.
3. Shop for the "fresh stores", get them aboard and stowed.
4. Pick up the plastic water containers that had been frozen overnight, and get them into the ice chest.
5. Pack suitcases for shipment home.
6. Pack duffel for the race.
7. Clean up the apartment and recover deposit.
8. Return the borrowed car.

9. Arrange for shipment of Vernon's car and baggage to Honolulu.
10. Top off fuel tanks and depart.

We worked our way down the list as the day went by and, somehow or another, accomplished the tasks and were ready in time.

Again, Vernon would drive to Los Angeles and meet us at the Yacht Club. Terrill, who had to drive her own car home, would meet us there in the morning to pick up Vernon's car for delivery to the shipper. Vernon assured us he would make this one, and we took in lines and departed at about 5 p.m.

We were a happy crew. It was great to have the tedious, frustrating period of preparation over with and be on our way. To celebrate after we cleared the harbor, we opened a bottle of champagne, and passed it around.

Craig even took his turn while I, the supervising uncle, figuratively looked the other way.

The trip up was uneventful, at least so it seemed. At one point while Joe had the hatch to the space under the cockpit open, he noticed an occasional bit of water welling out of the top of the rudder shaft housing. We concluded it was only a result of the force of the propeller turning, and would be no problem when under sail. We forgot it. We were to remember it soon, and with a vengeance.

Vernon was on hand to meet us as we were directed to a slip at Los Angeles Yacht Club. We tied up and then piled into his car, except for Gordo, who was to meet a friend, and went out for our last meal ashore.

Sleep was not easy that night. We were much too excited.

CHAPTER V

July 4th finally came. It was gray and still when we awoke. The sounds of life gradually grew in volume, however, as crews awoke, and as family and friends arrived to see them off.

We prepared our breakfast aboard, cleaned up, stowed utensils and suddenly could find nothing to do but wait. I made a tour of the harbor to wish my fellow skippers from Hawaii well and returned to Anuenue. Terrill arrived with friends and picked up the keys to Vernon's car. We visited and waited.

Ten o'clock finally came, and we decided it was time. Kevin dashed forward to place a wilted carnation lei over the bow of Anuenue and we took in lines. We would not toss them ashore again until we were snug in Ala Wai boat harbor. There I, too, would tie up at the Transpac mole after this most glamorous of all glamorous races.

There was still not a breath of air. The copper-colored water of the outer harbor lay flat and dead under a solid overcast, as we powered out of the inner basin. Up ahead and fanning out on either side, the wake of another Transpac contender broke the stillness of the harbor as it flowed across the surface in a wide "V" to either side.

The solitude didn't last for long. As we approached the harbor exit, yachts of all shapes and descriptions began to appear to port and to starboard, all headed toward the same passage to the sea.

We hoisted our "G" flag to the starboard spreader as we left the harbor. This was our identification and would allow us entry to the starting area.

The ocean between us and Point Fermin was already filled with yachts, some with sails, some without. Some with identity flags, some without -- contender from observer was difficult to distinguish. Overhead, aircraft buzzed the sky full of sound, or beat the air to an auditory froth with helicopter blades as their occupants watched the activity below.

I sent Jorge to flip on the radio. The rules allowed us to check in by this means. The speaker boomed back a garble of words against background noise. Voice against voice vied for the attention of "committee boat". I called Vernon to the helm and went below to take the mike. Jorge was fine with the radio, but I feared his Spanish accent would be lost for good in this potpourri of sound.

I waited and waited for a door in the wall of voices to appear. Finally I thought I detected one. I thumbed the button and said: "Committee boat, this is Anuenue checking in—over."

I released the button and the flow of reports from other skippers filled the cabin. No word of acknowledgment—nothing. I waited.

Soon there appeared another small break in the barrage of words and I pressed the button again. "Committee boat, committee boat, this is Anuenue checking in—over."

I released the button. The flood of conversation continued.

I wondered if our radio was working. Joe called down to remind me that FCC regulations required that I wait three minutes between calls. I waited.

I began to wonder if I was real—if this was true, or if I was just dreaming as I had been for twenty years about my presence here. I looked out. The ocean about was filled to overwhelming. We were off Point Fermin. The committee boat must be near. I turned back to the radio and began my vigil again. A momentary pause appeared and I pressed the button.

"Committee boat, committee boat, this is Anuenue, this is Anuenue, we are checking in— over."

I hadn't caused a ripple in the flow of messages from my competitors. I listened, hypnotized and isolated.

My thoughts flashed back—It was in the later 1930's—I didn't remember just when. I had come to the Islands just a year or so before. I was working for

"Castner Ford" in Wahiawa—I had been sent to Honolulu with a car full of employees to help bring back a shipment of new cars which had been off-loaded onto a pier in the "downtown" area. There, at the pier, moored alongside, was a sight that captivated me immediately—long, sleek, white-painted hull—shiny teak and mahogany topsides, tall varnished spars—I had walked along the pier just looking and longing. As I passed her stern I read from the golden letters emblazoned across her transom *Manuiva*. I asked about her and learned of the Transpac then. She was beautiful—she rose and fell with the sea as though she were a part of it, and I knew from that moment that I too must become involved with the wind, the sun and the salt of the sea.

I learned later what the "Transpac" was—I remembered a fleet tied up at Kewalo Basin, the name *Morning Star* came to mind and I remembered her being towed into Kewalo in the dark, after finishing off Diamond Head when—at first—only the silver of her long low hull could be identified behind the tow boat. Then, as she came into the lights of the harbor, her tall, tall spars appeared as if materializing from nothing, reaching up, up and up into the constellations of the Hawaiian sky. She was magnificent.

The following morning, or a few mornings later, I had gone to the harbor to see the rest of the fleet. I remembered—I fell in love with *Sea Witch*—her wide comfortable, sea-kindly beam—the lathe-turned posts of teak supporting the shiny rail around her cockpit and the long saucy bowsprit canted skyward as if to say, "There—there's where the wind is." It took me months to get over her.

There were other names and other loves, some too far away to reach for—like: *Queen Mab*, *Java Head*, *Chubasco*, *Nam Sang*. There were *Legend* and *Staghound*: and my mind flashed back to the radio. Out of the jumble of sound came the words: "Committee boat, this is ———, (I didn't catch her call letters). Anuenue has been calling you to check in, did you read her? Over."

And the committee boat answered: "Affirmative, Anuenue is checked in."

I did exist.

It was real.

We were here.

I never learned who by benefactor was. I thank him now. He brought me back to reality.

I returned to the cockpit and ordered the mainsail up. When it was hoisted, it hung limply from the mast, rippling gently from the flow of air we created as we powered on.

We finally identified the committee boat as it appeared for a fleeting moment in the forest of Dacron. We turned to seaward to search for the flag at the other end of the line. We found it, and turned back.

My watch read 11:30.

I closed the throttle and turned off the ignition. It was time to put rubber bands around our folding propeller to keep it closed. This would present the least possible surface to the flow of water as it sped astern during our passage.

Joe was ready to go over the side. He had confessed to me earlier that he had volunteered for this job in the belief that one of the younger crew members would be shamed into doing it. None of our warm-blooded Hawaiian juniors had come forward, however, and Joe was left to perform the feat himself.

He stripped to swimming trunks, stepped over the lifeline, turned his back to the water and pushed off. It was something to behold. He rose instantly from the chill water and looked at us with glazed eyes as he clutched at the side of the boat. He took a deep breath and dived below the surface. He was up in a moment and literally walked up the side of Anuenue and back into the cockpit.

I ordered up a large towel and a bottle of brandy. Joe had earned the first "shot".

His eyes turned to me and his blue lips mumbled "It's cold."

I could believe him. I, too, preferred my water from down where the trade winds blow.

A measure of my own excitement can be taken from what followed.

My mind immediately snapped back to positioning for the start. We were not where I wanted to be. There was insufficient wind to get us there. I reached down, turned the key and pressed the start button. The engine sprung to life. Joe looked at me aghast as Vernon dove for the switch and cut it. He turned to Joe and said: "It wasn't in gear, it's okay."

All I could think was: "I may put on a cool front, but Oh, boy!" -- I had completely forgotten the bands around the prop.

We ran the genny up to capture as much as we could of the two-to-three knot breeze that was coming in from the southwest and reached slowly for the flag at the Catalina end of the line. We found it again, circled it and tacked back towards the California coast where the committee boat was lost in the scrum of sails.

The big Canadian ketch, *Mir*, drifted alongside and a crewman called to us: "Which way do we start?" "This way?" and he pointed to the north, "Or this way?" and he pointed south.

"This way I think," I called back pointing north.

I immediately began to question my own response. I sent Joe below to determine the compass course to the west end of Catalina. I assigned Gordo to keep his eye on the flag and asked Kevin to find the committee boat.

I had been wrong. Catalina lay in a direction requiring that the line be crossed toward the south. I hoped Mir's navigator was doing a bit of checking for himself.

A voice from the radio informed us that the 10-minute preparatory flag was going up.

We drifted slowly to the north. Time was almost stilled.

We had drifted only two hundred feet back of the line when the authoritative voice from the radio announced the white signal down and, 30 seconds later, the blue signal up. I came about and headed for the line.

We were in perfect position. The ocean was full of boats, but none was within two hundred feet of us and we had clear air, what there was of it, all the way to the start and beyond.

We moved slowly down the line as the seconds ticked into minutes. Within a boat length of the line, the voice from the committee boat announced: "Stand by for a countdown to postponement—ten, nine, eight, seven, six, five, four, three, two, one, mark."

I couldn't believe my ears. I cried: "What'd he say? What'd he say?" Only to have confirmed what I feared I had heard.

My thoughts were of protest, protest, protest, but the omnipotence of the race committee is not to be challenged in such matters.

I came about again with resignation and started back across the line. The whole fleet was on its way up to my end, and, to make the situation worse, the committee granted a second ten-minute delay just to give them a chance to get there.

When I turned to "run" for the line for the final time, there was barely enough water left to float Anuenue. There were boats packed solid to port and to starboard as well as ahead and astern. If I could have seen the flag, I could have walked to it without getting my feet wet. I could only hope the whole mass would move with me because there was no spare surface left in this part of the ocean.

Two big "A" class boats, their masts reaching up to clear air above the fleet, moved up to windward of us. As they drifted by, the breeze curling around their sails, back-winded my genny and forced me slowly over onto a port tack against the helm which I was holding hard over. There was a Cal-40 not more than six feet away to my right and I was bound to foul her. As I looked toward her in desperation, I saw the same backwind take control of her genny and we "pirouetted" together without making contact.

As the big "A" boats cleared us, we turned back, again, a duet, and sailed on slowly across the line. We were like "solid-pack tuna" curled up in the middle of a can.

Jorge popped up from the cabin to inform us that the radio had reported a protest against *Windward Passage* for barging. We looked for her, and spotted her on port tack heading north up the coast.

It was a good fifteen minutes before I could find room to come over onto a port tack and go searching for clear air. As soon as I found room, I came over and headed off after *Windward Passage*. I didn't see her again however until I arrived at Ala Wai.

As soon as we were in relatively undisturbed air, I ordered the genny replaced by the lightweight reacher. It wasn't as flat, of course, but I felt its weight would keep it flying better, and thus give us more drive in the zephyr we were contending with. It did quite well. We were pleased to see that we were pointing better and footing almost as well as *Rascal*, a large Class "A" boat. Joe said: "If we can stay close to her, we're in the money."

A little later, still beating up the coast on a port tack, the 73-foot sloop *Pursuit* started coming up from behind and to weather of us. I ordered sheets tightened a bit, pointed Anuenue up and we climbed easily above her track before she passed, thus avoiding the turbulent air she left to leeward. My Rainbow was behaving beautifully even though she had been "cheated" out of a good start.

Our plan was to tack as soon as we could lay a line near the west end of Catalina. In the murk, the coast of California disappeared long before we could see the offshore island. We watched the veterans we could identify, and when they began to come about we followed.

The wind slowly picked up and swung to the northwest, so we re-set the genoa and began searching the ocean in a vain attempt to locate our Hawaiian competitors.

There were sails everywhere. It was impossible to tell where we were in the fleet but the radio soon began to report boats rounding Catalina. The big "A" boats were first, of course, but we were amazed, and didn't know whether to be pleased or chagrined to hear that *Dakar*, another N/41 from California, was the fifth boat around.

She must have had clean air at the start. We could barely see the outline of Catalina.

Before the race, we had been anxious to run a check on our knot meter to determine its accuracy. We had never had the opportunity, but it was about to present itself. I had just handed the helm over to Joe to get some relief, and, as I stepped up into the forward section of the cockpit, I saw someone waving frantically from a large power boat astern. As it drew near, I recognized Dick Lindsey at the wheel. There was a camera man at the rail clicking away at us busily.

I called to Dick to check our speed. He finally got the message over the roar of his engines and pulled alongside to pace us. We checked out together at six knots. Not bad for a beat in light winds I thought, now to set about making up the time we had lost with our bad start. Dick asked for the whereabouts of *Americana* and *Hawaiiana* to which we had to report no knowledge, so he headed off in search of them.

The radio continued reading the roster of the fleet as boat after boat passed Catalina. I was afraid to count. I feared the number would reach too far down the list before we arrived.

The outline of the Island clarified, and the brown cliffs and valleys solidified as we drew near. We were coming in well above Arrow Point not far from the west end.

As we approached the Island, I noticed a sloop coming up from my port side. It had a familiar look about it. My first thought was this is great, we're ahead of him, but as it drew near I recognized Taffy Sceva's Islander 37 *Roughneck II*. My spirits fell again. She was Class "D" and we gave her time. I did have some sailing to do, if that grand reputation was to be created.

I crossed "Taffy's" bow, ran on in toward Catalina for a few hundred yards and came about to beat on up to a position where I could tack again and clear the end.

Shortly after I tacked I started to hear a call -- "Hey, Stu!"

I looked about and there at the wheel of a vaguely familiar power cruiser was an ex-Commodore of the Waikiki Yacht Club, Cliff Spencer. Cliff had left the Islands a year or so earlier to pursue his business interests in Southern California. We had a friendly visit across the span of water between us. I pointed out "Taffy's" Islander to him and as he turned away to continue his Island visit, I read the name *Sunbeau* across the stern of the cruiser.

She should have looked familiar. She had been moored in Ala Wai for many months, and had performed committee boat duties for Island races a number of times. Her owner was a member of Waikiki Yacht Club and had been traveling the Pacific when I'd last heard of him.

It was a nice touch of home just before our last ties with land were to be severed.

We beat on up the short distance remaining until we could come over again to starboard and clear the rocks off the west end. As other boats up ahead tacked over and crossed our bow, we did get an emotional lift. There, not three hundred yards ahead, was *Hawaiiana*. There was still a sizable fleet behind us. We weren't too far back after all.

As the rocky point drew toward a position abeam, I came about again and started after *Hawaiiana*.

It would be a sweat, I thought as I looked ahead at the nasty water churning around the rocks at the west end. I had tacked short and, if the wind headed us at all, I'd have to take another hitch.

My practice in "pinching" Anuenue up into the wind on the occasion of the Sunday warm-up race a week earlier stood me in good stead now.

She would lose speed, but I knew she would climb. We hardened sheets to the limit and I held her up. We cleared the churning water by a scant fifteen feet. The crew held its collective breath and everyone stood as lightly as they could on the deck as we went by.

After we had passed, Vernon commented: "Well, I'll bet we've set a record for going by the closest."

Up ahead, a quarter of a mile or so, stood another large rocky formation reaching up what appeared to be a hundred feet or more into the sky. The first sight of it brought hearty laughs and a quick scramble for cameras from our crew. It strikes me now as a symbol of what "Lady Luck" had to say to us although we weren't to know the full truth of the message for some days yet. The base of the rock looked like the back of a large hand. The fingers on either side were folded over and a large central finger pointed straight up into the sky.

We cleared it, started our log, and headed out into the Pacific.

CHAPTER VI

Back in Honolulu, at one of our crew meetings, we had worked out a watch system that would move the members of the crew around the clock, leaving no one with a more favorable schedule than another. There would be two daytime watches—6 a.m. to noon —and noon to 6 p.m.—followed by three nighttime watches for four hours duration each. This way, each crew member would move forward a watch every twenty-four hours.

I had spent a good deal of time going over in my mind the strong points of each crew member in an effort to arrange for strengths to balance and thus give the best possible combination of skills at any moment. It was not an easy task. There were many unknown quantities, for none of us had worked together over such an extended period.

Personality and spiritual strengths must also be considered. Living in each other's "hip pocket" so to speak, keeping bunks warm as watch after watch tumbled out and tumble in, was bound to fray nerves when fatigue began to take its toll.

I didn't arrive at a final decision until the day before the race. When I did, I called my crew together and made the assignments.

Craig and Gordo would be assigned to Joe. This watch would be on duty at the start and would be relieved at six o'clock by Vernon, who would have Jorge and Kevin with him.

I explained that I would be actually on duty from the start until we cleared Catalina and that Joe and I would share the helm during this most important leg regardless of how long it took. I knew the excitement of the start would make sleep next to impossible for the off-duty members but I encouraged them to rest when they could. The tension was bound to subside as watch followed watch, and spirits had to be kept as high as possible, with sufficient rest, if we were to be a racing crew. It would be easy to maintain a high pitch of attention while competitors were in sight and we could measure the results of our efforts by our relationship to them; it would be difficult with nothing but the ocean and the sky available for reference as we made our way down the invisible sea lanes toward the finish line. The only indication of progress, other than an anticipated gradual change in weather, would be the slow march of "X's" across the chart when daily positions were computed and plotted.

There would be some jolt to spirits, good or bad, each morning at 8 a.m. PDT as the roll was called of the fleet and positions were reported. The radio would become the only link with our competition and the world outside the confines of Anuenue, unless we chanced across a fellow yachtsman on the broad expanse of ocean ahead.

• • •

As Anuenue cleared the last rocky sentinel off West Catalina, we cracked sheets a little to pick up drive. It was just after 5:30 p.m.

Vernon got out our shore-prepared dinner and we ate it heartily. We had been too busy to remember lunch.

The fleet was scattered, some boats holding above us, sheets still in hard, and others falling off to the south.

Six o'clock came and Vernon with his watch took over the running of the boat. The wind was picking up, and the sea was getting lumpy as darkness crept up behind us.

I ordered a course of 220 degrees magnetic. I wanted to hold up close to the rhumb line for the first few days, so I could fall off a little as the wind moved after and get a "chute" up as soon as possible. 220 degrees was about as close as I could hold in the increasing blow with the sheets cracked.

At 9:30 p.m., I went below for a nap.

I woke up at about eleven o'clock to the sound of wind whistling through our rigging and the feel of a heaving, confused sea under our keel. The weather report given us before our departure had been accurate. It had predicted winds upwards from twenty knots on a line between Santa Rosa and San Clemente Islands. We had reached that line and the wind was there.

I began to feel what command meant as I stood in the cabin pulling on my foul weather gear and watching the action in the cockpit.

Earlier, before going below, I had refused a request to have the cockpit dodger raised. It offered excellent protection in the forward end of the cockpit where a crewman could retreat after his stint at the wheel, but it presented more surface to the wind. While we still had the wind from ahead, I didn't want it slowing our progress.

Joe was standing in the cockpit eyeing the sails aloft, the salty brine covering him periodically as Anuenue buried her shoulder in a swell and threw the top of each back over her decks, drenching the exposed crew. Behind him, on either side of the wheel sat Craig and Gordo, both heads hunched over the lighted compass, all four hands clutching the wheel, pulling and pushing constantly in unison, in an effort to hold the course I had set.

Joe saw me as I emerged and said, "She's a bear to hold. I've had two men on the wheel for the past hour. One can't handle it."

"It's my turn to go on," he continued and he stepped back to the wheel, tapped Craig on the shoulder and signaled Gordo to go forward.

Gordo let the wheel go and moved away as Craig slid from the starboard seat to the one on the port, and Joe settled down to starboard. The two of them then continued pumping the wheel as the wind and the seas tried every ploy to round Anuenue up into the wind.

Gordo plopped down on the cockpit seat -- exhausted.

We had been told she would be hard to hold on a reach, but this was something I truly hadn't expected.

How long could we hold this pace I wondered.

• • •

I sat in the lee of the cabin and watched—and thought. As we heeled to the gusts and surged with the seas, —and struck the waves blow after blow with our bow, I was reminded of my first ocean race in a "ship" under my own command. *Dee Jay* was a salty little ketch. She was all of eighteen feet long on deck with thirty inches of bowsprit pointing the way ahead. I had committed myself to her some four years before this first ocean race quite on a spur of the moment.

I was a labor negotiator. My company had been in negotiation for some time. It was during a period after we had made a proposition to the union and were awaiting a response. The wait might be three hours—it might be three days. I had gone out for lunch, and on the way back, I passed a bookstore and noticed in the window the book "Boat Building in Your Own Back Yard". I bought it and took it back with me and began pouring over the plans. This is when I found *Picaroon*. She was designed as a sloop without the bowsprit. Her beam was seven feet six inches—a fat little pigeon—and she reminded me of my early love, *Sea Witch*. I doodled with design, as the hours passed, and soon she was *Sea Witch* in miniature. On my first trip home, to seal my commitment, I went by the lumberyard and ordered the oak and cedar to complete her hull.

I was living at this time on the Island of Maui far from the source of marine supply; consequently, I learned much about improvising in the matter of boat building during the next three years that I worked on her in my own back yard. I was, however, employed by a large sugar plantation that was blessed with complete machine shops—even a brass foundry. Among other chores, I made the molds for her heavy pintels and gudgeons in my own home shop, and had them poured at the foundry. I melted and poured the lead for her keel; cut and sewed her sails according to the instructions from another book, "Sailmaking Simplified". I even made some of her blocks for running rigging from leftover fiberglass cloth and resin, which material I had used to cover her hull and deck.

The only structural failure she suffered during the five years I sailed her was a broken swedge on her backstay. This I had ordered made up in Honolulu.

This first race was after she had spent a year patiently teaching me to sail her in the water around Maui. I entered her in the annual Labor Day race from Lahaina, Maui, to Honolulu. On the morning of the event there were black squalls marching in solid ranks down Pailolo Channel between Maui and Molokai. Molokai was completely hidden as we started in winds of twenty-five to thirty-five knots. We were over on our ear and soaked to the skin in minutes. We soon reduced sail to jib and mizzen and went plodding down the "slot" watching the larger boats disappear over the horizon ahead. Our one real competitor, the twenty-two foot sloop *Shady Lady* was unable to make time in the heavy going, and so she accompanied us in the "tail-end Charlie" position until a broken stay forced her out at Kaunakakai, Molokai, about three hours after the start. We were to learn later that Kaunakakai was a relatively peaceful haven for about a quarter of the fleet that had been forced out of the race with broken gear. We, however, took all the weather had to offer; ran on down the "slot", crossed Molokai Channel and finished off Diamond Head some eleven hours after the start. This was "blazing" speed for my eighteen-foot pigeon, but it was so late that the race committee had already left the finish line and retired to the bar. We learned later that they had assumed we had given up and checked out at Kaunakakai with the others.

The only loss we suffered on that trip was one seat cushion that floated out of the cockpit while we were heeled over a bit too far, early in the race. The Coast Guard had picked that up and returned it to us later after we were back home on Maui.

I knew "Anuenue" was a thoroughbred and could show well in a race, but I fervently hoped she was made of the same stuff as *Dee Jay* had been, —it was beginning to look as though we would need stamina as well as speed.

• • •

A half hour passed and the game of musical chairs started again. Craig moved out, Joe moved over and Gordo moved in.

I felt a strong urge to move into the game and take some of the load off the crew, but reason told me these conditions could last some days. This is the first night, I thought, if our crew can't handle it on a regular watch basis, we are through as a racing yacht. There will be plenty of relief needed later, I must not move in and help now.

I felt like Captain Bligh, as I continued to watch them heave and pull at the wheel.

Another half hour passed and Joe rotated off again.

I had checked the inclinometer at the navigator's station below. It recorded our angle of heel as swinging between 30 and 35 degrees. Dick Lindsey had told me that the designer recommended holding the angle at 25 degrees or less for best results. She would slow down if she went beyond that, he had said.

We were still carrying a full main and the 150% genoa. We discussed changing down to ease the load at the helm. I didn't want the crew worn out the first night, and I wanted those below to get as much sleep as possible. Joe and I decided we could turn a reef into the main without help from the off watch crew. I got out the crank for the roller reefing gear, and handed it to Joe who by now had on his safety harness. I put mine on and we crawled forward over the heaving deck to the base of the mast. After fifteen minutes of struggling, with Joe throwing his body into turning the crank as I let off on the halyard, we had rolled it down to the extent the jack line would allow. We crawled back to the cockpit snapping our safety lines ahead of us as we went.

When we had put away our harnesses, I called to the team at the wheel and asked, "How's that?"

Gordo looked up from the compass, water streaming down his face and mumbled, "Better -- some", -- and he turned back to his heaving at the wheel.

I checked the inclinometer. We were back up a bit, swinging between 25 degrees and 30 degrees. That would have to do until daylight, I thought.

Joe's watch continued, one man pulling from starboard, one pushing from port and one resting. As two o'clock approached, the crewman on rest went below to awaken Vernon and his hearty seamen. There ensued calls to which we were to become accustomed from the darkened cabin, "What? not already!" "Who's got my jacket?" "Where are my boots?"

Soon, however, the new crew was on deck and ready to take over.

Joe discussed the problems of his watch with Vernon and went below to fall into his sack forward.

I stayed on for awhile, my concern growing as I watched the new crewmen fight through their turns at the wheel in the cold flying spray, while I sat in the lee of the cabin house.

Jorge, even in the dim reflected light from the compass, was beginning to look a little green. His jaw was clenched, however, determined that he would not let the sea get the better of him.

I sat through a couple of hours of the watch and then retreated again to my bunk.

Getting to bed required some doing—taking off foul weather gear was a risky business in these seas. The usual method of getting out of such a garment was fine on a solid foundation, but under these conditions, in the confines of a darkened cabin, struggling to keep the wet outer surface from dampening the dry inner surface it was something else again.

First, there was the simple problem of just standing upright without using hands for maintaining a balance. In my corner of the cabin this took some gymnastics. The chart table was at my back, banging me in the ribs, and the galley was before me creating an abyss in which to dive if caught unprepared.

I gave up undressing in a dignified manner after a few tries, and sat on the deck for the whole operation thereafter.

I don't believe any of us, however, undressed beyond removing foul weather gear for the first three or four days. It was a bit chilly for our Hawaiian blood, and the effort was just too great.

As skipper, I had pre-empted the quarter berth located aft of the navigators station to starboard and extending back under the cockpit seat. Sleeping, head forward, feet, aft, I was handy for a call from the cockpit hatch when needed. The only major problem was that it was next to impossible to crawl into this berth feet first while the boat was heeled over on a starboard tack. The head of the berth extends out into the cabin and there is nothing handy to hold on to while curling feet and legs up to get them into the opening back under the cockpit seat. I gave up this practice also after a few days and just crawled back in headfirst, a much simpler operation. The crewman wanting my attention would just have to come below and wiggle my foot.

• • •

I awoke to a gray and windy dawn. Vernon had taped the week's menu to the cabin bulkhead above the stove and was heating water for coffee. No one was particularly interested in a hearty breakfast. As I crawled out of my bunk, he turned, pointed at the inclinometer and said: "It's back up again, shouldn't we do something about it?" I looked at the indicator ball rolling slowly back and forth in the curved glass tube between the 30 degree and 35 degree marks. "We'd better get the mule up," I said, "before your gang sacks out."

I dressed in my oil skins and boots and went on deck to take the wheel during the sail change. Jorge went forward in the cabin and, with Kevin's help, got the heavy mule out of its bag and heaved it up through the forward hatch to waiting hands above. Joe was on the bow in the pulpit, and he snapped it into the stay as Craig and Gordo passed it to him. We got new sheets led forward and then dowsed the genny. It was a wild, flogging monster coming down. The crew forward finally tamed it and lashed it securely along the lee rail, the mule was snapped to the halyard and hoisted. “That’s better,” Vernon called from the cabin hatch once it was up and drawing. “We’re back up around twenty-five.”

Joe’s crew came back and took over the helm while I, having softened during the night, ordered the dodger up. The hands available were more than willing to comply with the order. I noted a sly smile here and there as the job was accomplished.

One man could now handle the helm, but it was a back-bending job, and 30 minutes at a stretch was enough for the strongest of us. As I watched the members of the crew at work, or at rest, I noted the pale green pallor of sea sickness creeping into the ruddy complexions of most.

Almost everyone was suffering at least a touch of mal de mer. Some, I hesitate to name names, were able to hide all but a gentle convulsion, as they peered intently through the rail down at the water rushing along the side of the boat. Others, unable to conceal their discomfort, wailed openly in the effort to releasing the pent up pressures within them. I hoped it wouldn’t last too long—I needed them.

Joe interrupted my reverie as he called, “It’s eight o’clock—roll call’s on.”

Vernon and I dove for the radio as Joe flipped it on. I opened the navigator’s table and rummaged through for the sheaf of papers listing the entrants in alphabetical order. I found it, pulled out a sheet and slapped it down on the table. Joe grabbed a pencil and started recording. The communications vessel,

Bonhomme Richard, call name, *Bonnie Dick* was already on the air.

The plan was to call each racing yacht in order. The yacht was to answer giving its latitude and longitude, the wind velocity and direction at its location, and the barometer reading. If there were any special messages, the yacht was to so indicate; these were to be relayed after the roll call.

Anuenue came early in the roster. I took a quick look at the log. It recorded 128 miles. I adjusted the dividers against the scale on the chart, set one point at the west end of Catalina and stepped the other point down the track we had followed. I read: "Latitude 32 degrees 15 minutes north. Longitude 120 degrees 35 minutes west." I placed an "X" on the chart at the intersection of the coordinates, jotted down the figures and grabbed the microphone as Anuenue was called. I thumbed the button, announced my latitude and longitude and reported the barometer reading and the wind at twenty knots from 325 degrees true.

Joe and I both, I believe now, regularly judged wind velocity at lower than it actually was. Reliable reports of that first night and day indicate velocities of up to thirty-five knots. My log indicates we never reported winds of over twenty knots. Both of us, I imagine, had listened to too many tall tales around yacht club bars of high seas and high winds and were leaning over backwards to avoid being classified as "tall tale-tellers".

Bonnie Dick would pause in her roll call now and then, as particular names came up, and inform the fleet of casualties that had occurred during the night.

When she was finished, she had reported six contestants withdrawn and returning to the California coast. Two had lost masts, three had bent bowsprits, and, to my great dismay, *Bonnie Dick* reported *Roughneck II* skippered by my friend and confederate from WYC, Taffy Sceva, as turning back, but gave no reasons.

I called our escort for particulars and was informed that some steering problem along with "crew fatigue" was the cause. The report was hard for me to accept; steering problem, yes, but "Taffy" and his crew, most of whom I knew, wouldn't abandon a race after some twenty hours because of fatigue.

I didn't have to accept it. The receiver clicked as a button was punched and Taffy's voice came through the speaker, "This is *Roughneck II*, negative on that last report. *Bonnie Dick*, we are not suffering crew fatigue— we have lost our rudder."

The story of *Roughneck II* is one that should be told. Taffy returned to Newport, steering with sails and whatever other means his ingenuity could contrive. There he had his rudder replaced and started out again.

We were attending the Transpac Awards Dinner in Honolulu after the race when proceedings were interrupted with the announcement of a radio message from Taffy. Six hundred miles out of Los Angeles he had lost his rudder again but was running on down the trades under reduced canvas and "jury rigged" steering. He predicted arrival within a couple of weeks. He arrived as he had predicted and brought *Roughneck II* right to the front step of Waikiki Yacht Club with his emergency "sweep". He and his crew stepped off to as big a celebration as any yacht in the race enjoyed. They had earned it.

• • •

The roll call, and its auxiliary verbal traffic, was followed each morning by the weather report. In Honolulu, some weeks before the Transpac, a member of the U. S. Weather Bureau staff had conducted a series of seminars covering weather observation, cloud formation, wind patterns over the Pacific and mapmaking and reading.

The weather information came to us in a code of five digit numbers. We had been given a book of maps at the skipper-navigator meeting in L. A. before the race, and translating the five digit numbers gave us coordinates for plotting lines of constant barometer pressure, and fronts of one type or another that were present in the northeastern Pacific area.

It was generally agreed that the Transpac was a "weatherman's" race. As in any race, one needed a good boat and a good crew, but, if you could keep in the wind all the way down and avoid being entrapped by the "Pacific high", you had a good chance of being in the running.

The "Pacific high", an area of high barometric pressure, was characterized as a windless waste of glassy water where a yacht could drift for days with sails hanging limp and useless. From the edge of the high, the air moves outward in a clockwise spiral, increasing in velocity where lines of equal barometric pressure draw closer together. The location of the high is not constant; nor is its shape, intensity, or size uniform. It generally, however, lies somewhere on a direct line to Honolulu, but we were told, it could move north without notice leaving a direct route open; or it could expand and enlarge without warning, reaching down to snare anyone who wandered too close, in its trap of windlessness. It was considered good practice to keep at least eight millibars of pressure between you and the high.

The weather code that was broadcast to us each morning was made up from information collected at 5 p.m. PDT (Pacific Daylight Savings Time) the day before. Lady Luck got in her "licks" good or bad, through this opening in our defenses. We were working with information some sixteen hours old and setting courses to where we wanted to be twenty-four hours hence. We could go south to a safer, longer route or we could tempt the "Lady" and cut close under the high for a more direct, short way to the finish line.

This first morning we weren't particularly concerned about too little wind—we did have to concern ourselves, however, with what the future held in store for us. Joe took down the code, plotted the information and we had a look at it. It indicated no need for going any further south. The wind had already backed toward the north a bit, so I ordered a course change to 240 degrees magnetic, paralleling the rhumb line home.

We retrimmed sails for the new course, and I had just settled down in the cockpit when Joe, who had gone below, called from the hatch, "Stu, you'd better come have a look at this."

I joined him in the cabin. He lifted aside the stairway from the cockpit, which also constituted a hatch to the space under the cockpit deck, stooped down and pointed. I stooped beside him and looked along the line he indicated. From the top of the rudder-post housing on the lee side, a stream of water was flowing. It slowed as Anuenue swung to a more nearly upright position and gushed as she heeled over from a starboard swell. A little babbling brook flowed steadily down the bottom of the hull toward the bilge.

I crawled over the boxes of spare parts, compounds, fastenings and tools to make my way back for a closer inspection. There was a bronze plate around the rudder shaft, bolted with three small bolts to a flared-out flange at the top of the housing. The water was flowing from a gap of approximately one-quarter inch between the plate and the flange. I called for a wrench. Joe rummaged through the boxes and handed me one. He crawled back with me and snapped on a flashlight directed at the fountain head. I found a piece of nylon cord of the type we had used to lash down our emergency rudder. I wrapped it around the gap several times and then tightened the nuts all around as much as they would go. The plate came down, perhaps a sixteenth of an inch, but the flow of water was unchanged. I suggested a rubber sealing compound we had laid in for just such an eventuality. Joe found it, handed it to me and I started squeezing it from the tube into the offending space. It would hold and set up on the high side, but as I worked around the rudder post into the area of the flow, the water from the leak kept spitting it out creating a black "gooey" mess all over my hands and the hull beneath.

We had purchased a two-part epoxy compound before departing. The label on the can indicated it would "set up" under water. We decided this might have enough body to stand up against the flow of water, so Joe dug it out of the "goop" box and handed it to me along with a putty knife and a paper mixing cup. I mixed the two parts together and started pressing it into the gap with the putty knife. It came out as fast as it went in and joined the black rubbery mess on the hull below. I called for a roll of gauze from the medical kit. Joe pushed open the hatch and asked a crew member to bring it. When it was delivered, I buttered several feet of it with the compound and wrapped this around and around the offending opening. The water came through as before. We covered the gauze with tape, and it came out around the edges. We finally encircled the whole bandage with hose clamps and screwed them down tight. The clamps stopped the water coming from the gap -- it now came, at exactly the same rate, from up around the rudder shaft. We couldn't bandage this -- the shaft had to turn.

We finally came out of the compartment under the cockpit floor convinced that we had a leak to contend with, and that we'd better start contending by other means. I lifted the cover to the bilge and found water, sloshing back and forth with the roll of the boat, right up to the cabin sole.

Our engine was located off center on the port side. Access was gained by lifting a cover under the after seat to the dining table. Joe had removed the seat cushion and was lifting the hatch as I leaned over to take a look. The water was half over the engine, and as we heeled further to port with a beam sea, it completely covered the carburetor located on the port side of the engine.

My thoughts flashed back to the night before. At one time, during the wee hours I had gone below to check batteries and found them low. I had ordered the engine started to charge them.

The engine has a horn with a horrible wail, wired in such a fashion as to give warning when something is not functioning properly. The horn would begin to sound as the ignition was turned on, but would stop the moment the engine started, if all was going well. On this occasion the engine started right off, but the horn continued to wail.

Thinking of nothing but the sleeping crewmen below, I dashed to the engine, threw back the cushion, opened the hatch and began feeling around for the horn. I could well remember the incident because, in the process of feeling around, I had put my hand into the spinning alternator fan. Fortunately I had gloves on and sustained only bruised fingers. I had finally found the horn, found a wire running to it and had yanked loose the connection. The wailing had stopped, but as I thought of it now, I was chagrined to realize I had failed to understand the message I had been given. Something had not been right with the engine.

It was still not right. It was, in fact, much worse. We would be fortunate, indeed, I thought, to get it in operation again. I immediately crawled over to the long port side seat, now used as a bunk, and called for all our buckets to be brought. As they arrived, I began dipping into the engine compartment, filling them and passing them to hands waiting in the passageway. They were then emptied into the cockpit, where their contents would run back into the sea, and brought back to me for refilling. While I was so occupied, other crewmen started dipping into the bilge to remove the water from there. I bent, dipped, filled and passed; bent, dipped, filled and passed. Slowly, ever so slowly, we made headway against the flow of water that had collected below.

We had two hand bilge pumps. The intake for one was moved into the engine compartment and a crewman started pumping. We finally had the bilges dry. Vernon checked the time, it was 5:30 p.m.

Joe and I had gone under the cockpit floor at about 10 a.m. that morning.

I was tired.

I had no doubt there were others a bit worn down. Vernon had been running the yacht while Joe and I had been trying to control the leak. Watch schedules had ceased to exist.

We settled down where we were—Vernon leaning over the engine from the passageway where he had been taking full buckets from me and handing me empty ones, Joe across the table next to the bilge hatch where he had been dipping and passing buckets. I was still kneeling on the head of the leeward bunk next to the engine compartment.

Vernon said:

"I think we should make a decision." He walked over and looked at the log and returned. "We're 185 miles out. I don't doubt we can control the leak. We've emptied over a day's intake in an hour and fifteen minutes. If we keep ahead of it we can handle it. But, I don't think we should go on without instruments and radio. If we can't get the engine started, we'll be without power to run them."

I turned to Joe and said:

"What do you think, Joe?"

He replied:

"Well, I'll have to have a look at the carburetor. Maybe we can get it cleaned out and start the engine."

I thought back to the many times I'd sailed between the islands at home. I must have worn a groove between Lahaina, on the Island of Maui, and Honolulu. Most of this had been with no electric power other than the dry cells by which I lighted the running lights. Vernon had not had this experience, and I could understand his concern.

I was not particularly concerned, however, about a lack of electric power. The log was very handy for navigation. The wind guide was particularly helpful at night when "telltales" were hard to see. We had spare running lights. We were racing.

As I reported, I was very tired and in need of sleep.

I said: "I'm too tired to make a decision now. I'm going to sleep a while, and we'll talk about it later."

I fell back on the bunk and was asleep almost at once.

When I awoke, Joe was wiping out the last bits of the carburetor parts and assembling the pieces. Within a few moments he had it together and reconnected to the engine. Back in the galley area, Kevin was just finishing his stint at the pump. The pump squealed pitifully as the plunger was pushed in and pulled out. No amount of lubricant would still it, as we were to learn.

Joe said: "Let's give it a try."

Vernon was standing by the companion-way. He called to Jorge at the wheel and said: "Turn her over."

The starter motor whined in its klaxon-like way, and the engine fired. It ran a few seconds and stopped.

Joe reached down to the choke control beside the engine and said: "Try it again."

Vernon called to the cockpit again, and again the starter motor whirred. The engine started, then slowed. Joe pumped the choke. The engine revved up and settled down to a steady purr.

We were in business. There would be no need for any major decisions.

CHAPTER VII

We sailed on through the night of July 5th and into the morning of the 6th, still under reefed main and mule, the squeal of the pump punctuating each rotation of the crew on watch.

The dodger had improved conditions in the cockpit measurable. We were able to put out seat cushions and keep them reasonably dry and the man on "rest" could stretch out on the low side in relative comfort, out of the wind and flying spray.

By morning, the wind had moderated somewhat and continued to back slowly toward the north. The seas were still confused from the winds of the 5th. The solid gray overcast remained unbroken, and a dreary dawn came slowly from astern, spreading gradually over us to the horizon ahead as the 6 a.m. watch change approached.

At the change, with all hands available, I ordered the reef rolled out of the main and the genoa re-set. We were booming along in grand style.

Just before eight o'clock I checked the log in preparation for the morning roll call report. It read 273 miles. I stepped this off on the chart with the dividers and placed an "X" at 31 degrees 10 minutes, north latitude, 123 degrees 5 minutes, west longitude. The barometer read 1014.00 millibars and I estimated the wind at 15 knots from 350 degrees true.

Sea sickness was subsiding, and crew morale was improved with more stable stomachs. As a result, excitement arose when roll call started and we began copying the position reports of our rivals.

Hawaiiana had failed to respond to her call the morning before, so we listened intently as her name came up on the roster. Again, no answer. We wondered aloud if something serious had happened to her, or if she was just playing a game with *Curioso*.

Curioso's sailing master was noted for his failure to respond to the roll call, and we didn't expect to hear from him until he was safely across the finish line.

When the roll call was finished and we had plotted positions of the boats in our class, we were more than elated. We had the lowest handicap in Class "C", yet we were up in the middle of the fleet. This should put us in a good handicap position, I thought. We were about 15 miles ahead and 15 miles north of *Americana*.

It was beginning to look like the weather was made for our shorter rig.

The sixth of July continued -- just an ordinary, peaceful, average Sunday. I searched the heavens for a break in the clouds at noon in the hope of getting a latitude position, but the overcast was so solid there wasn't even a hint of the sun's whereabouts.

We did face one problem, however; the engine continued to give us trouble each time we tried to start it to charge batteries. Joe would dissemble the carburetor again and blot more water out. He'd reassemble, we'd restart. It would run along fine for awhile, and then, for no apparent reason, suddenly die. The starter motor itself, of course, was a heavy drain on the batteries. We found we were having to charge five times a day to keep our voltage indicator out of the "red" area on the dial. I am no electrician, but this struck me as an inordinate amount of drain for the power we were using. To conserve, we outlawed the use of cabin lights. We would use flashlights. There was a good supply of batteries for them, or so we thought at the time.

Joe disconnected the indicator and instrument bulbs in the switch panel to save what power we could there.

Before leaving L. A. harbor on the morning of the start, Fred Smales of *Americana* had suggested we meet, on the air, each evening at 6:30 to exchange conversation and experiences. Up until now, we had been too occupied with other duties to remember until well after the time had passed. We remembered early this Sunday, and started the engine a half hour before the appointed time in order to have the batteries well up for the occasion.

Americana responded to our call, and we exchanged pleasantries and commiserated over each other's problems. *Americana* was having her share of the latter. She too had a leak, but had stopped it. Much more serious, the housing around one of the shivs leading the steering cable to the quadrant had broken under the load of the helm. They had been under emergency tiller during repairs. Cy Gillette, well-known in yachting circles in both Hawaii and throughout the Mainland, was a member of *Americana's* crew. He had spent his own hours under the cockpit floor effecting the repairs.

This interlude was a pleasant release from the confinement of our own small universe. We would remember the appointment hereafter, although it was to become the undoing of us insofar as electric power was concerned.

Vernon prepared dinner. Most of us were eating with relish now, and we settled down for another long night. We were still under genoa and main. The wind was still from slightly ahead of the beam at about 15 knots.

I continued to crawl into and out of my bunk. I was crawling in head first now. It was much easier that way. I was trying to bridge watches, so that I was available during each watch, if needed. I had not yet found it necessary to relieve anyone for serious cause. I did relieve occasionally, both to keep my hand in and to offer extra rest to a tired crew member. It was still only the night of the 6th, and we had almost nineteen hundred miles to go. The crew must settle into a regular schedule and be able to maintain it.

Entering my bunk head first was like crawling into another world. I was usually sleepy before I went down, but I was left, each time, with a considerable amount of noise-sorting to do.

The starboard quarter berth is enclosed on one side by the outer hull, and on the other side by a partition separating the bunk from the area under the cockpit. The after end is walled by a partition just below the main boom traveler in the cockpit. The forward end is the entrance, just aft of the navigator's seat.

The space was like the inside of a ukulele. It was a large sounding box, magnifying the sounds from the surrounding areas. From the outer side there came the constant sound of the sea rushing by the hull, punctuated occasionally by the loud slap of a wave breaking against the side of the boat. When a wave broke into the cockpit, there were the sounds of disconcerted crew members speaking their minds about the sea. I could even hear the gurgle of the water as it flowed through the drains back into the ocean. The main sheet traveler, being just over my head, could really attract my attention when it banged over and against the stop, as a result of an accidental jibe. It was like the crack of doom. I could sort out the grinding of the chain across the sprocket in the steering mechanism and I could hear the steering cable rubbing the edge of the holes through which it led down to the quadrant.

There was a thumping noise that puzzled me for several days. I was much relieved to finally discover that it was made by champagne bottles rolling against the side of the icebox located across the under cockpit compartment opposite me.

I went through my noise-sorting process each time I crawled into my bunk and I slept much better when I was able to identify all sounds that I heard.

• • •

Life aboard a small racing yacht consists of more than just tactics and the mechanical problems associated with the boat and its auxiliary equipment. As I mentioned earlier we were sleeping in each other's bed, living in each other's vest pocket, so to speak. As skipper, it was a part of my job to be aware of personal conflict when it arose, eliminate the cause, where possible, or smooth the edges of raw nerves by any means available if they threatened the efficient running of the boat.

It has been said by the experts in long distance racing, that the second to the fourth day out is the "spiritual" low period of a race. The excitement of the start holds spirits high until fatigue from the lack of rest sets in. It then takes a day or two for everyone to become accustomed to the idiosyncrasies of his shipmates and the routine of watch keeping.

I confess, I was too preoccupied with mechanical problems and the evaluation of crew members as helmsmen, or as pure "sailor men" to notice the living problems that were developing. The first one became evident the night of the 6th.

The marine "head" for a small yacht is by nature a cantankerous, obstinate, infernal machine at its best. Most of them, I am sure, were designed under the spiritual supervision of the devil. Many a boat, I know, has sunk at its moorings at the mere whim of its head, reacting, I feel certain, to the nature of the life it has had to face at sea with uninitiated guests aboard.

An uninitiated guest, I grant, can be a problem. A "call" to the head by one is not generally accepted as subject for genteel table conversation. As a consequence, the guest makes his call, performs his ritual, and then finds he is faced with a mechanical monster that will not respond at all to his usual means of appeasement. Being embarrassed by his failure, the guest then leaves his offering and retreats, leaving the owner or the crew to bring final satisfaction to the unappeased head. After many years of sailing, I am firm in my belief that no guest who is too genteel to accept instruction in the operation of the marine head should ever be invited aboard a yacht.

The head on Anuenue is like most heads in racing or cruising yachts. There is first a valve that turns on or off like a faucet. Most heads have such a device in one form or another. Second, there is a pump. If the valve is turned on, the pump brings in water from the ocean during its upwards stroke and expels it from the bottom of the bowl on its downward stroke. When the bowl is completely flushed, the valve is closed, and water no longer comes in. After a few strokes the bowl is completely empty, a good way to keep it in a heaving sea.

One other mechanical point: the contents, in being expelled does not go directly downwards into the sea, but first goes through a tube which leads upwards until it is clearly above the waterline of the boat, and then downwards and into the sea. This device is necessary to keep the sea from backing up and filling the inside of the boat, a most unsatisfying eventuality.

On the evening in question, while most of the crew was assembled in the cockpit finishing dinner, Joe burst from the head, and in a tone not to be challenged, said: "Hey, listen you guys! The stuff in that head has gotta go up at least two feet or it'll come right back into the bowl and spill all over the deck. It'll take at least ten strokes of the pump to get everything up two feet and leaving nothing but sea water in the system." "Then," he continued, "you close the valve and dry the bowl. I can hear the pump from where I sleep, and I'd better be able to count ten strokes."

I may have been guilty myself, but I agreed with Joe's sentiments wholeheartedly and seconded his motion with the suggestion that a good round dozen strokes of the pump wouldn't wear it out before we got home.

The next blow fell the following morning at watch change, just before breakfast when, with good cause, Vernon said, also in firm positive tones: "Listen, I want everyone to know I didn't sign on this boat as cook. Before we started it was understood that the oncoming watch would prepare the meal, and the watch on duty would wash the dishes. I've been doing most of both and I'm getting tired of it. It's about time," he continued, "we settled down to regular duty."

He also was unquestionably right. Vernon and his boys had stashed the food. He knew where it was from the record he kept of its whereabouts. The rest of us had been leaving it to him not only to dig it out, but to prepare it as well. I vowed from that moment to pay closer attention to the performance of all duties aboard Anuenue, and not just to the ones having to do with her speed through the water.

The crew took both blow-ups from the watch captains in seamanlike fashion and were better for it from that point on. There was just one other incident that required my attention.

My son-in-law, Jorge, loved sailboat racing and was prone to let his "hot" Latin blood get the better of his tongue in his excitement when things didn't seem to go as they should on the foredeck, or wherever else he was helping work the boat. When I began to notice some resentment to his vitriolic pronouncements, I called the crew together to remind them that we had a boat to race and that we would race it better if we all worked in harmony in deed and in word. I assured them that there would be no problem we couldn't face, and that we would solve all problems more expeditiously in calm discussion than by any other means.

The speech appeared to be accepted as delivered and tensions eased as a result.

At roll call Monday morning, July 7th, we reported our position at 30 degrees 15 minutes north latitude, 126 degrees 45 minutes west longitude. The wind was still at 15 knots from 330 degrees true and the barometer was rising slightly to 1014.5 millibars. Our day's run, by log, was one hundred and ninety miles, not bad at all considering we weren't yet in a position to surf on a following sea. When we could get a chute up, with long steep swells boosting us along, I felt sure we would be over the two hundred mile mark regularly. I was in for some disappointment.

The roll call positions for the fleet were copied and plotted on the morning weather chart for study. We were still looking good in fleet standing, and the weather chart provided no reason for a change in course. The wind was still ahead of beam on a course of 240 degrees magnetic. We continued on, under genoa and main, wishing the winds back so we could set a spinnaker flying and start the long slide downhill toward home. The confusion in the sea pattern was abating, and the long regular swells following down the wind line were developing.

By 10 a.m. our wishing was beginning to pay off. The wind was backing rapidly toward the north. I ordered Anuenue up into the wind slowly, as I watched the wind guide. It recorded the apparent wind at 90 degrees on a heading of 260 degrees magnetic.

This should be enough, I thought. We can fall off to 220 degrees or 230 degrees, put up a chute, and even with our increased speed the apparent wind would stay aft of abeam. I called, "All crew on deck, bring up the 1.5 chute and let's get it set."

Jorge went quickly forward for the spinnaker.

Craig dove into the rope locker, grabbed sheets and started leading them.

Joe was already in the bow rigging the spinnaker net.

Vernon, Kevin, and Gordo dropped the dodger forward to clear space for action, snapped snatch blocks into the rail aft, and began sorting out sheets, guys, and the pole lift, clearing each through its leads to a winch where it could be manhandled.

At 10:15 we were ready.

I ordered "up chute" and it came snaking out of its bag in the pulpit and up to the top of the mast. It hung limp in its stops for a few seconds as Kevin hauled in on the after guy to bring the clew to the end of the pole and pull the pole back from the forestay. As the end swung back, the stops gave and the chute opened with a resounding pop.

"It's beautiful," I thought, as I felt Anuenue surge forward, but immediately the bow started swinging rapidly to the starboard and up into the wind as I tugged at the wheel to hold it back. I could hardly turn the wheel; I jumped to the left side of the cockpit, braced my feet and started hauling on it spoke by spoke.

We were already up into the seas and over on beam ends to port, with the spinnaker filled off to the left, holding us down.

"Let the sheet run," I called.

I had the wheel hard over now, but she wasn't responding.

The crew forward had grabbed at whatever hold was handy as we went over, but they were now scrambling back to the cockpit to lend a hand.

As the sheet played out, the spinnaker collapsed and began flopping wildly in the wind. With the pressure off, Anuenue began to respond to the helm and she slowly turned back onto course. The foredeck crew hadn't had time to douse the genny. I ordered it down while the spinnaker flogged the air, feeling sure this would ease the helm and make her manageable.

The boys got it down quickly, and before they had finished lashing it to the rail, I called for the spinnaker sheet to be hauled in and the chute reset.

Kevin ground away at the winch, as Joe and Gordo hauled in on the "tail".

I headed off a little further to about 220 degrees magnetic.

The chute filled. Anuenue surged forward and started her turn up again. I was quicker this time, jumping to the left, bracing, and hauling in on the spokes of the wheel.

It was no use. Around into the sea and wind she went and over to port she heeled, floudering like a wounded gull in the seaway, her chute flapping like a great broken wing.

We would just have to wait for the wind to move further aft, I thought. It's obvious we can't carry a spinnaker on a reach in these winds and seas.

I ordered the chute doused. The crew fought it down and stuffed it into the hatch.

We set our reacher and staysail. It took some time getting them trimmed to my satisfaction, the reacher sheet hauled outboard to the end of the main boom, and the staysail sheeted into the port rail. When they were set and we were sailing again, it was noon. We had wasted an hour and forty-five minutes and had lost at least a dozen miles, a loss we could ill-afford. My logbook, in good Hawaiian pidgin English notes the occasion with the remark:

"10:15 - Tried 1.5 chute —no can!"

"12:00 - Set reacher and staysail."

Anuenue charged along with the wind and sea striking her from just aft of the beam. We were back on a heading of 240 degrees magnetic and fighting, but controlling, the helm.

The sun was breaking through the clouds occasionally so I handed the helm over to the crew on watch and went below to check the nautical almanac for the time it would pass our "assumed" meridian. (I hadn't obtained a celestial observation since the start.) If we were at, or near, where I thought we were, in so far as longitude was concerned, the sun would pass our meridian at 13:33 PDT; we were still using Pacific Coast time, as roll call, weather, and other communication media were scheduled according to the time in that zone.

I tuned in our portable radio to the wave length where I had been receiving time signals, borrowed Vernon's watch, since mine had not been keeping time properly, and checked his watch error. As the time of local noon approached, I started shooting the sun and checking the sextant reading.

The sun reached its maximum altitude at approximately the time I expected it would. Our longitude would not be far off, but, of course, this shot would only confirm latitude.

I went below and ran through the work sheet.

When an answer came out at the bottom, I'm sure my eyebrows, such as they are, rose a bit. I started at the top of the work sheet and step by step went deliberately through the computations again.

The shot had been good, I knew.

The computation was without error.

We were 66.2 miles south of where I had assumed we were.

That was a "far piece", and it was quite a shock for a fledgling navigator.

Joe came below with me and we checked over our chart. This provided some comfort. The chart showed current observations that had been collected over the years, and a calculation of "drift" in the ocean area we had passed through accounted for approximately half the error. The remainder must have been, in part, leeway because of the beam seas, and, in part, helmsman error in reporting "course made good".

I could understand, with the struggle we had steering, how it would be a temptation to run off downwind now and then to ease the pressure on the helm.

I would have to pay closer attention.

I cautioned the watch captains to do likewise.

The sun, which had ducked behind clouds soon after my noon shot, reappeared about two and a half hours later, so I went for my sextant again and called off the shots to Vernon, I took three fast ones, computed the results, advanced my noon shot according to the log reading and the compass course and came up with my first fix at sea. At 15:47 PDT, we were at 28 degrees 46 minutes north latitude, 127 degrees 14 minutes west longitude. It was good to know just where we were, at least once in a while.

The afternoon wore away, and Jorge started preparing dinner. He, or one of the other crewmen, would have done so anyway, regardless of Vernon's earlier pronouncements, because this was a special occasion. It was Vernon's birthday, and Jorge had planned for it before he left Honolulu to fly up for the race. Jorge might have a Latin temper that could flare up at the slightest provocation, but he also had a real flair for remembering the things that would please.

Dinner was served. As I remember, it was ham, one of Vernon's favorites. It was followed by a birthday cake with one lone candle. The cake had been saved all the way from Newport. We cracked a bottle of wine, brought along especially for the occasion, presented a few gag gifts, and then for the finale, Jorge brought out his tape recorder, set it up and turned it on!

Vernon's mother lived in a large house across the street from his home in Wahiawa, a few miles inland from Honolulu. With her lived her sister, "Auntie Glad", and their mother, "Nonnie", who was ninety-six years of age at the time. Nonnie, beloved by all the generations of her brood, had been failing rapidly following a fall, and was confined to the local hospital.

From the tape recorder, came the voices of the three "girls" wishing Vernon a happy birthday and to us all "God speed" on our way home.

It came near to breaking Vernon up. He retreated quietly to a corner of the cockpit after the tape had finished and sat in meditation for several minutes.

• • •

We missed our radio rendezvous with *Americana* that evening; we were late as a result of preoccupation with our own social schedule, and when we tried repeatedly to call through, they failed to answer.

Batteries were low when we gave up, so we struggled with the engine again, and finally got it going before we sucked them completely dry. The engine continued its practice of stopping suddenly in the middle of a steady run, but we finally completed the charge.

We had spare, dry-cell operated, running lights aboard—a requirement for the race, so I loaded them with batteries and rigged them to port and starboard to remove this load from our electric system.

We saw our first signs of company on the broad expanse of the ocean this night. As I came up to join the 2:00 to 6:00 a.m. watch, Vernon pointed out a stern light ahead, some distance off the starboard bow. He said he had spotted it shortly after coming on watch and that we appeared to be overtaking it steadily.

It's amazing what a little company can do. The crew members off the helm were wide awake. They would stand up every few minutes to peer intently at the lone light. As they sat down again, they began to speculate as to who it might be.

I noticed that the wind had moved back a bit so I had them ease sheets slightly.

The light ahead moved across our bow to the left and slowly drifted back towards our port beam. I could see the strangers starboard light at 05:00..

I called Kevin: "Bring up the big light. Let's see if we can find out who it is."

Kevin answered: "Right," and went below to fetch the large flashlight.

I pointed it in their direction, flashing it at them for a moment, then up at the mainsail, lighting our sail number.

They obviously had no problems with electric power. In a few seconds, lights appeared from two masts glowing over their entire upper rigging. She was a schooner and a large one. She was running under headsails and mainsail only; there was nothing rigged from the foremast.

I went below to thumb through the Transpac program, and I made a quick examination of the pictures of all entries. There was only one schooner, *Queen Mab*, and what we had seen didn't resemble *Queen Mab*

I suspected it was just a casual meeting with a stranger in the night, and this is what it proved to be. Dawn came soon, and our "fellow traveler" was still in sight, not far astern. She was clearly a stranger, and so she still remains. She did, however, brighten up one watch for us and break the monotony of a turn at the helm, a turn at the pump, and rest.

Our eight o'clock position report on the morning of July 8th showed a twenty-four hour run of one hundred and eighty miles, ten miles short of the day before. That would be the mileage we lost laid over on beam ends trying to fly the chute.

I couldn't afford to give away another ten miles, but I couldn't win a downwind race without using a spinnaker while my competitors were using theirs.

At ten o'clock I ordered the 2.2-ounce storm chute out, and within a few minutes, we had it up and flying.

I had the helm and, so long as I was quick and put all my "beef" into the wheel the moment she started to round up, I could keep her on the track. We began to surf in grand style, and the crew members were elated to watch the knotmeter pass the end of the dial at 12 knots, as we caught a long, sliding ride down the front face of a wave now and then.

It wasn't all "peaches and cream" however. Every few minutes a cross-sea would strike the stern from further toward the quarter and around she would go. Sometimes I could catch her before she lost her momentum and bring her back on course, but when she got too far around, we would have to spill the wind from the chute to get her straightened out and then refill it. I felt sure we were making reasonable progress, however, and not losing too much by rounding up, so I turned the helm over to Joe and went below to prepare for a morning shot at the sun.

I was sitting at the navigator's table making my preparations when I heard a resounding crash followed by a loud flapping of the spinnaker. I jumped into the cockpit and spun to look forward.

There, like a javelin thrown by a giant hand, was our sixteen-foot spinnaker pole protruding from the after side of the mainsail about two feet above the tack. At least six feet of the pole had come through. It was waving about madly as the spinnaker, now out of control but still attached to the other end, beat the air to a froth.

The crew didn't need to be called; the members were already on deck.

We let go the after guy, and ran it out. The pole stopped its thrashing, and we doused the chute.

Jorge and Gordo went forward, extracted the pole from the mainsail and put it back in its brackets. I went forward to join them and to see what had happened.

Our spinnaker car on the forward side of the mast was a fitting about ten inches long. It had two large eyes, into either one of which the pole could be clipped. The second eye would be used in a two-pole jibe, for setting up the second pole which we carried, before the first one was taken down. The fitting also had smaller eyes angled out at about 45 degrees from either end. These were used for attaching the line by which we controlled the height of the car on the mast. They were to come in handy later.

The eye that the spinnaker pole had been clipped into had disappeared completely. There remained only the jagged base where it had broken away from the body of the fitting.

I called to get the reacher up, while we restopped the spinnaker; there was nothing to be gained by contemplation now. There would be time for that once we got moving again.

We reset the reacher, the staysail was still flying, and we got her under way again. We sailed well with this rig, but we didn't have the "punch" to surf that we had with a spinnaker up.

Joe and I discussed the broken eye in an attempt to find a reason for it that we could control. He felt that it might have resulted from letting the outer end of the pole get too high, thus bending the eye with the inner end. I wasn't convinced this was good cause. I don't believe Joe was either. We finally "marked it up" to a bad casting, and I ordered the 2.2 ounce back out and set again, with the pole clipped into the remaining eye.

Handling the helm continued to be a hand, and back, killer. It required an immediate response to the feel of the sea.

I had been watching my helmsmen closely.

Jorge and Gordo had been sailing with me a long time and were good solid crew; I regretted now, however, that I had not given them more time at the helm in Island races. These races were usually of short duration as compared with this one; the competition was keen and close. I had hung onto the tiller except for short periods of relief. They hadn't had an opportunity to pick up the "feel" necessary to react before Anuenue started to swing, and this was waiting too long.

Vernon, in the year we had sailed together regularly in the Newport 30, had advanced considerably, but most of this practice had been in the relatively flat water in the lee of Oahu off Honolulu. He had too little time in a big following sea to be at ease under the conditions we were facing. He needed more time and experience, and I hoped to see that he got it.

Craig was a question mark. He too was short on experience. He was developing a good "feel" and so long as his attention remained constant, he could learn to handle Anuenue under spinnaker in these seas. My concern had to do with his dedication to the job. He was young, and I feared "fun" could turn to boredom without warning, and attention would be lost. As the wind and seas moved aft, inattention would allow not only excessive rounding up but could produce an accidental jibe, and this we could well do without.

Already he was having difficulty waking up and staying awake for his night watches. I knew how he could "put out", no matter what the demand, for football and wrestling. I was afraid sailing was just not that important to him, and I needed dedicated Corinthians on the wheel. Perhaps I remembered my own boys, Jere and Dennis, too well at this age. They loved to sail with me, if I were going somewhere; but just to go sailing?—no, it became boring too soon. I recalled again that early first Lahaina to Honolulu race in *Dee Jay*. I had a friend as crew, a competent sailor, and the two boys. It had been a stormy trip, with black squalls all along the route. All day long I had to keep ordering Dennis, who was then only thirteen, off the cabin top and below. I was afraid he would go overboard in the event of an accidental jibe. He would stay below for awhile but would soon be out again sitting on the cabin top in the way of the boom. Jere was sixteen, Craig's age, and also had a good hand on the tiller. I had him on the helm as we entered an area of steep breaking seas just off Koko Head.

He had been doing fine, but, a moment of inattention, and we were over into a jibe followed by the broach of all broaches. Both booms banged over, and Dennis, who was out on the cabin top again, dove under the main and grabbed the gunwale. *Dee Jay* had her spreaders in the water. Before the race I had wondered if we had cleaned the bottom well enough. As *Dee Jay* righted herself, Dennis turned to me from his sprawled position along the rail and said: "Hey Pop, there's no grass on the bottom of the keel.

• • •

I decided I'd better not push Craig into the duty roster for spinnaker work.

This left Joe, Kevin, and me. Joe and I, of course, had a good bit of experience, having raced our own boats a number of years. Kevin, as I had expected took to the helm immediately and had the strength to respond at once. I could tell by watching him that he could feel what he was doing—that he could, and did, anticipate and act before Anuenue got her head around. He qualified quickly as a full-fledged helmsman under all conditions we met. Kevin was a happy, good-natured young man, always ready to perform at his best.

We sailed on through the 8th and 9th of July following much the same pattern. We would get the chute up the first thing in the morning, rotating Joe, Kevin, and me through the turns at the helm, and throwing in Vernon and Craig as frequently as conditions would permit. In the late afternoons, as fatigue set in from fighting the helm all day, we would reset the reacher and staysail and go through the night with the regular watch schedule.

Morning roll call still showed us in the race, but it soon became obvious that the other boats had set their chutes and left them up. The leaders were beginning to pull away from us.

• • •

It was the night of the 9th, I believe, that Gordo got his whale, although my log isn't clear on this point. I wasn't convinced myself until some days after we were home that such a monster was involved.

I had gone down for a short rest, sometime in the middle of the night. I had crawled back into my sound box, identified all noises I heard and had gone to sleep.

I was awakened with what sounded like an anvil being struck by a sixteen-pound hammer within inches of my ear.

I shook the sleep from my eyes as I backed out of my burrow.

Anuenue was heeled to starboard.

The cause of the "clang" I had heard came to me; we had jibed, and the main sheet traveler had come across from port with the force of the wind in the mainsail behind it and struck the stop just above my head.

I normally awoke immediately on such occasions without too much "fuzz" in my head, but I must have taken a few extra seconds this time, because

I missed a part of the explanation of what had happened. It wasn't until we were at home that I was made fully aware of the cause of the jibe.

At the moment, and for the next day or so, I heard the crew kidding Gordo about hitting a whale. I assumed it was their way of relieving his embarrassment for allowing the jibe.

It wasn't.

As Joe reported to me later, Anuenue was booming along on a broad reach at her usual eight knots when all of a sudden she struck something. Her bow was pushed to port, slewing her stern around to starboard. This had caused the jibe.

Joe said that he had looked over the side as a large "cloud", gray against the black of the ocean, drifted slowly astern. He had not been able to discern the shape, but the only logical conclusion he could reach was that it had been a whale sleeping on the surface.

Months later when we hauled out in Honolulu, we discovered a "chip" had been broken away from the bottom of the rudder.

We put Anuenue back on starboard tack, dug out a new rubber shock band for the boom vang and rigged it, to replace the one we had broken when we jibed, and settled back down for the night.

Gordo finished his watch, but he had obviously been shaken by the incident, and did not look forward eagerly to those turns at the wheel in the pitch black nights thereafter.

CHAPTER VIII

At 8 a.m. on July 10th, our position was 26 degrees 30 minutes north latitude, 135 degrees 35 minutes west longitude. We had averaged only one hundred seventy miles per day for the eighth and ninth of July; we had done better before the wind had moved aft, and even though we were getting some twelve-knot-plus surfing runs, with our spinnaker, we were still spending too much time over on our side recovering from a "knockdown".

Bonnie Dick had begun reporting the leaders each morning after roll call and we were clearly not among them.

I must confess, I was frustrated. I had a boat with "go", and I couldn't control it.

That morning at dawn, I know I passed some of my frustration along to the crew when I made a sudden change in orders.

The last few days, we had been setting the chute at dawn with the 6 a.m. watch change, and carrying it as long as we could—that is, as long as we were standing up more than we were over on our beam ends. This morning had started the same way. We had the chute rigged in its bag forward and were hooking in the pole when, on sudden impulse, I ordered:

"Belay that, snap in the reacher sheet, we'll bring that across and boom it out."

Joe looked at me in surprise, and I'm sure—disapproval. I mumbled something about "smelling" more wind coming and wanting to try a storm rig for downwind.

I'm still not sure why I made the change; I'm only sure it was on impulse, not carefully thought out, a result of my disappointment with our progress.

As it happened, it's just as well I made the change when I did, we were to need a rig that would make steering easier soon, for more reasons than one.

My log book for the morning of July 10th carries another short entry of note. It reads: "7/10 —0700........switched water tanks."

Anuenue had two bilge water tanks of stainless steel. The starboard tank held thirty gallons and the port tank forty. We had been pumping from the port tank because it was on our low side, and we wanted to keep weight to starboard at least until the wind was further aft.

I wasn't particularly concerned when I read the log book entry which had been made by Vernon. We were almost half way home with 1200 miles to go. We still had the other tank and the forty-five gallons in plastic containers that we had moved forward to ease our pumping chores. We could move those back soon, I thought; when the wind got well aft, we should be upright and the intake through the rudder shaft should diminish.

We ran through the early morning hours wing-and-wing, under main and boomed-out reacher. The wind was still from the quarter, requiring the pole to be fairly far forward, which didn't give us the best use from our sail plan, although it did ease the helm considerably.

By 10 a.m. my frustrations with progress were back on the other tack. We weren't surfing on the big ones, we weren't racing, we were just sailing. I ordered the crew out and the chute set. Not the storm chute—the big one. The wind was only in the 15-knot range. The boys got out the 1.5 ounce with dispatch, doused the reacher, and had it up in a few moments.

I was at the helm while Jorge was still forward tidying up sheets and the sails we had lashed to the rail.

Jorge suddenly cried out, "Let the after guy go."

I called back, "What's the matter? It's drawing fine."

He called again, with agitation, "Let it go! Let it go! Let it go!"

He must have sufficient reason, I thought, to be this upset about it. Gordo and Kevin were all ready on the sheet so I reached over, loosened the hitch on the after-guy and let it run.

We stuffed the chute into the cabin. Joe and Craig went forward to get the reacher out of its lashings and back up, as I turned the helm over to Vernon and went forward to see what all the fuss was about.

Jorge was just snapping the pole back into its deck brackets; he didn't say anything, he just pointed at the spinnaker car.

The remaining eye had broken loose on one side. It was twisted up like a corkscrew, it's jagged end pointing an accusing finger at the top of the mast, from which the spinnaker had flown.

I don't know what had kept the pole from flying out again and spearing another hole in the mainsail.

Jorge was forgiven for his sudden assumption of command from the foredeck.

Joe and Craig got the reacher back up and trimmed. Joe joined me at the base of the mast and we had a short conference. We concluded that we could attach the spinnaker pole to the pad eye on the side of the mast to which the reaching strut was normally attached. This would do for booming out a headsail, but it wouldn't do for a spinnaker.

To put our conclusion into practical use, we re-rigged the spinnaker pole from the starboard pad eye, snapped the starboard reacher sheet into the outboard end and hauled it across. The reacher filled to starboard and began to draw nicely.

There was still a good bit of air slipping through between the mainmast and the forestay. To capture this and put it to work for us, we hoisted the genny to port and trimmed it to the outboard end of the main boom.

We had just created what was to become known as our "fore quadrilateral", or "spider web". It worked fine, but there was a very narrow range, with the wind from the quarter, within which we had to steer to keep all sails full. If we steered up a little high, the boomed-out reacher would back and start beating as it luffed; if we fell off too far, the genny would be blanketed by the main and start popping in its low key. At the proper angle however, all sails would draw and we moved well.

Once we had the rig set, I called a meeting of all hands in the cockpit.

"We have to be able to fly a spinnaker," I said. "I want any and all ideas."

I held the useless spinnaker car in my hand for them to see.

"Now, come on, let's have some thoughts," I added.

The gang produced.

Ideas began to form, and were proposed.

I don't know—nor is it important—who came up with the final solution. We worked as a team and, within thirty minutes, had devised a new spinnaker car that stood up with no problem for the remainder of the race.

We got out the hacksaw, cut the car in two between the two broken eyes, turned the pieces end-to-end and ran a stainless steel shackle through the two small eyes that had been used to attach the line with which we controlled the height of the car on the track. We ran a second shackle through the first, and had our eye into which we could snap the spinnaker pole. We mounted the newly-conjured car on the track, tied the control lines into the broken "corkscrew" eye and pushed it up to position.

Within a few minutes we had the fore quadrilateral down and had the small chute flying.

We were quite pleased with ourselves, but yet another problem was beginning to show itself. My spinnaker helmsmen, Joe and Kevin, were beginning to complain of sore hands each time they moved in behind the wheel. I knew what they were talking about; my hands, too, were stiff and sore. It took a good ten minutes at the helm to loosen up the stiff muscles and the palms, bruised from struggling with the unyielding wheel, continued to hurt all through the watch. Even while they slept, I could see the signs of Joe and Kevin's overworked hands. They would sleep with their arms outstretched and their fingers hooked as though they had just come from around the wheel. The other crew members were suffering from the same problem, but not so acutely.

We took the chute down late in the day and ran up the twin headsails. The wind was up—we had obviously run through the front that had first appeared on our weather chart the day before.

I called the crew together at dinner time, and announced that I would like Kevin and Joe kept off the wheel for at least twelve hours to give their hands a chance to rest. We would run under twin headsails alone, I said, to ease the steering. They agreed wholeheartedly, and we set up a new watch schedule for the night.

We had a long chat with *Americana* that evening and discovered that they had broken out an eye in their spinnaker pole car also. We commiserated with them and warned them the other one would go soon. We passed along our solution to the problem for their consideration when the inevitable happened. When we finished our conversation, we noticed the batteries were particularly low, so we cranked over the engine for a recharge.

The engine continued to give us trouble, stopping in the middle of a run for apparently no reason. We would turn it over, it would start and run smoothly for awhile and then stop again. I was at the wheel and noticed a particular pattern to its stopping; it happened each time a steep sea caused us to heel sharply to port. To check my observation, I gave the wheel a sudden turn to starboard to heel us over to port and sure enough the engine died. We started it again and I called Joe. He came to the cockpit hatch and I said:

"Watch, I can kill the engine."

I spun the wheel again and it died.

Joe snorted and went for the tools.

He was gone for some little while, and I could see he was bent over the engine compartment tearing down the carburetor again.

When he had finished, he re-appeared in the hatch and said: "Start it again."

I started it and he said:

"Now try to kill it."

I gave the wheel a spin as before, but nothing happened; the engine kept purring smoothly.

"All right," I said, "tell me about it."

Joe had reasoned that, as we heeled sharply to port, the carburetor float would be pushed to the top of the bowl and that it must be sticking there, allowing the engine to suck out the remaining fuel in the bowl. It was dying because the float didn't drop with the fuel level and replenish the supply.

He was right. He had found the cause of the hang-up and fixed it.

Joe was a right handy man to have along.

We ran the engine on through the battery-charging cycle, but, when we cut it, one battery dropped down again almost immediately. As we recharged several times throughout the night, we still came up each time with one good one and one bad one. We would have to keep an eye on that, I thought. I was to remember the thought—and soon.

Dawn the morning of July 11th found my spinnaker helmsmen rested in body, but, by contrast, their hands felt worse. I canceled the morning spinnaker drill and had the main hoisted instead. To keep the sails full, we had to bring our heading up a bit, to 250 degrees magnetic. This would be all right. The heading was well north of the Molokai Channel, but we could jibe later and come back down. We had no reason to select a different course as weather reports were becoming useless. We would diligently copy the code each morning, but when we translated it onto the chart it showed a nice clear picture of weather along the Pacific Coast, and out about as far as we were—it showed nothing, however, of conditions between us and Hawaii.

We had begun toying with our portable radio each night trying to tune to the regular commercial stations in Honolulu in the hope of picking up more helpful weather information. We hadn't had much luck yet, although we had begun to receive Honolulu stations the night before. It had been quite a comfort for all of us to hear familiar voices and familiar call letters coming faintly to us from eleven hundred miles away. We had crossed the halfway point during the night.

I continued to hold one clear memory of this mid-ocean segment of our trip.

The Coast Guard communication plan for the racing fleet assigned responsibility to a California station for the first four days. Responsibility for the 9th through the 13th was assigned to "Ocean Station November". The remainder, until the fleet was in, was assigned to Honolulu. Our weather and emergency communication was to be passed on through these points.

"Ocean Station November" is a ship stationed at latitude 30 degrees north, longitude 140 degrees west. Its purpose, under normal conditions, is to collect and pass on weather information. There are a number of such ships stationed about the Pacific and the data they relay to shore stations is the raw material from which our weather charts are made. "November" was also a radio station from which we could check our position by means of our radio direction finder.

The thing about it that clings to my memory is the sound of the voice that came to us through our radio. There was a certain "out of this worldliness" about it. We listened to it at different times during the days or nights we were passing through the area; the men on board must have stood regular watches, but the voice always sounded the same, and somewhat like a robot. The speech was slow and deliberate with no sign of expression. There was a medium-pitched metallic hum behind it, and it seemed to echo faintly as though it were coming through a large, long metal tube. When we first picked up "November" on the 9th it was four hundred miles away to the northwest. Our closest point was during the day of the 11th when we passed it three hundred miles due south, and we heard it last on the 13th, from almost five hundred miles to the southwest. The metallic sound made that imaginary metal tube seem long and narrow at the start; it shortened and grew in diameter as we swung by to the south, and then, stretched out again, growing longer and longer as we drew away toward home.

It was a strange, lonesome, cold voice, even when relaying information relative to the removal of an injured crewman, from a yacht near us, by a Navy destroyer.

• • •

Roll call was coming soon after dawn now. We were still operating on Pacific Daylight Savings Time. Honolulu time was three hours later and we would soon have to begin changing our watches.

Our position was 25 degrees 15 minutes north latitude, 138 degrees 37 minutes west longitude, a twenty-four hour run of one hundred eighty miles. It appeared we were caught up in time and distance sequence. No matter what we did, we couldn't get out of the 170 to 190 mile rut.

• • •

Bonnie Dick had been communicating with one member of the racing fleet by code. The yacht's radio would not put out voice communication, but the click of its microphone button could be heard and this was used to relay its position.

I was still concerned about Jay Moore and his *Hawaiiana* crew. After roll call, I called *Bonnie Dick* and suggested they try another call to *Hawaiiana* and see if the same suggested procedure would get an answer. *Bonnie Dick* tried, but there was no response. Later, Fred Smales from *Americana* called and informed us they had received one short call from Jay with a message of troubles similar to ours. They had no power from the start, and were reserving such "juice" as they had for their final approach to Honolulu.

This conversation was the undoing of us. I was about to move, figuratively, into the same boat with Jay.

As I finished the conversation and snapped off the transmitter, Craig said, pointing at the voltmeter:

"Look, it just went down all of a sudden."

The meter needle was in the red. I flipped the switch from one battery to the other and then to both. It stayed in the red. I looked up at the recording log. It had stopped turning.

I know very little about electricity. I was going to be no help, but a team effort had worked before. maybe it would work again.

I announced to the crew that we needed any and all ideas. I cautioned them not to hold back any thought, no matter how unlikely it appeared on the surface—it could lead to a solution.

We produced ideas, many, but tried none this day. Joe, a usual, more knowledgeable than the rest of us in matters mechanical, said, that with rest, batteries would build up a bit, and he suggested they be given absolute rest for twenty-four hours. To be sure they got it, he disconnected them from the system.

We sailed on through the day with twin headsails, the two genoas, and the main. As we sailed we jotted down ideas to try for starting the engine. They included:

a) find something to spin in the wake as we moved along, and harness it to the alternator to turn it and build up a charge.

b) a similar device using the wind instead of the water.

c) pull the spark plugs and put some gasoline in each cylinder when we tried to start, so we could get an explosion with the first spark.

d) wire together every dry cell we had aboard to build up a charge.

e) rewire the batteries to double the voltage.

These and many other ideas were suggested for consideration if the batteries didn't produce after a rest.

We built up our spider web in the rigging as the day wore on.

The outer end of the spinnaker pole was swinging around a bit occasionally, even though the fore guy, the after guy and the topping lift were snug, so we ran an extra line through its outer eye and led it down to the rail to pull against the topping lift.

We had a vang set up on the main boom, but we had accidentally jibed again and broken another rubber vang strap. We only had one good one left, so we got out our "Band-it" tool and tightened a strip of steel around two overlapping pieces of rubber and made a new one. This we took forward and, using it as a shock absorber, rigged a preventor from the foredeck to the end of the main boom. We already had lines run through blocks on the end of the boom with which we hauled out the leeward head sail sheet.

It was quite a web, but it was producing mileage. We were surfing, making better then twelve knots at regular intervals as the big seas built up astern and boosted us along.

The wind was now blowing from the northeast, and, as the day progressed, big black rain squalls built up astern, marched slowly down the sea toward us and passed on ahead. Some marched over us, causing a scurry for rain jackets; they would pass over us, to port, or to starboard, leaving the ocean flattened for awhile from their downpour.

The wind would increase measurably during the time we were in or near a squall and we would "scud" along ahead beautifully. We played with the squalls all day, changing course as much as we could with our "web" to get into the edge of those that were passing near, in order to reap the benefits of their increased winds.

That afternoon, as a squall marched far off over the horizon ahead, the sun's rays bounced back a beautiful double rainbow. We were sailing into it.

"Anuenue" — Rainbow. This must mean well for us, I thought.

Gordo went for the movie camera and captured several feet of it on film before it faded and died.

Our ill fortune was not over, but in a few more days I was to discover the good fortune in that rainbow and it would be well received by all aboard.

The next morning, after I had plotted an early sun line, our spirits were lifted measurable when we discovered we had broken out of the rut. Our twenty-four hour run had been two hundred and fifteen miles. The boys had looked at me previously with suspicion and doubt in their eyes, when I had continued to report one hundred seventy or one hundred eighty miles as a day's run. I was not only skipper this morning — I was pal — I was buddy — I was Navigator Supreme.

July 12th was a day to be remembered, though best forgotten. We started by listening to the roll call. I did not respond when Anuenue was called. I couldn't risk draining a bit of power from our over worked batteries. Instead, Joe and I started to work pulling spark plugs on the engine. We intended to "lace" the cylinders with gasoline in the hopes of getting a small spark from the batteries. My assistance was a mistake. My wife tells me I have natural antipathy toward gasoline engines, and they towards me. She must be right, in fact at times, my feeling I fear, is downright hostility. To my mind, an engine is to serve one purpose and that is to run when one turns on the ignition and presses the starter button. For me they most frequently spit, sputter, balk or die, and that is not what an engine is for.

With the pounds and pounds of tools we had aboard, we had no spark plug wrench. Hereafter, when preparing for a race, that will go at the head of list number two.

I picked up a crescent wrench, tried to fit it around a spark plug which was buried too deep in the engine head, and I pulled on it. The wrench slipped, banged the spark plug and broke it in two. We had no spare spark plugs; that would go on the list right under the wrench.

My language for the next few moments does not bear repeating. The exercise was therapeutic however. I was working out my hostilities.

Joe looked at the broken plug, and then at me, in disbelief, as I retreated from the presence of this infernal monster.

In penitence for my blunder, I took the broken top of the spark plug with me, mixed some epoxy compound, buttered it onto the broken end, returned to the monster and glued the plug back together. Such is the quality of my mechanical craftsmanship.

Joe struggled as best he could with the materials and assistance he had at hand to get the engine into some sort of running order. He reconnected the batteries and turned on the master switch. The needle fluttered up to the border of red and green. It just may run on three cylinders we decided. I sent Vernon to the ignition switch and starter button. It was better, I felt, if I stayed out of reach.

Joe was standing by at the choke control as Vernon turned the switch and pressed the button.

There was one short growl of the starter motor — that was all.

Vernon turned off the ignition. Joe turned off the master switch, and we met in the cockpit for a conference.

It was agreed, with no sign of objection from Vernon or Joe, that I would busy myself with the sailing of Anuenue, while others, with more affinity for gasoline power, worked down the list of ideas we had propounded the day before for building up the batteries.

In the end, it wasn't me at all; it was the engine. It flatly refused to run for the remainder of the race. And just to show its spiteful character, when we had the batteries charged after our arrival in Honolulu, it started and ran as smoothly as a kitten purrs, for Vernon, glued spark plug and all .

The mechanical crew below worked throughout the morning until they had exhausted all practical ideas. At noon I called time-out for spinnaker drill. We got it up and carried it for a couple of hours, but the squalls began knocking us flat again as they went by, so we doused it in the middle of the afternoon and re-spun our web of lines for the twins and the main.

I decided to make *Bonnie Dick* aware of our problems, if we had power enough to reach her. I didn't want concern to grow for our welfare when we continued to miss roll call.

When I turned on the transmitter, I got no response from the light that indicated it was on. We may not be able to call after all, I thought.

I pressed the microphone button and called: *Bonnie Dick*, *Bonnie Dick*. This is Anuenue. Over."

She answered at once, so I gave her a quick rundown of our problem and told her we'd be off the air until we were in range of the Diamond Head finish line. She expressed her regrets, wished us well, and we signed off.

I haven't forgiven her yet for her failure to pass that message along to Honolulu. When we got home, we discovered that the Honolulu committee and our families knew nothing of our power problems. We were just another yacht that had suddenly stopped responding to roll call.

• • •

Gordo was preparing dinner when the next blow fell.

Vernon came to me in the cockpit and said, "the starboard water tank is dry."

I was shocked. “It can’t be,” I said. “We’ve only been on it for two days. We can’t have used thirty gallons of water.”

“It’s been leaking then,” Vernon said. “We’re sucking up nothing but air.”

I suggested he send a crew forward to move back the water in plastic jugs, and the other gear which we had moved there earlier to lift the stern.

I was in for another shock.

Vernon was back within a few minutes with dismay written across his face. “Most of the plastic containers are broken,” he said. “They were piled in with anchors and tools and have obviously been punctured from the knocking around we’ve been taking.” I called for relief at the wheel and went below for a look.

There were two two-and-a-half gallon plastic bottles that remained whole. The others had jagged holes in them. We salvaged perhaps two quarts from the ruptured containers. I set the crew members who were below to pumping on the galley pump and the pump in the head washbasin to draw out every drop left to be pumped, we opened up the bilge and rapped on the tanks with our knuckles. A hollow empty sound came back to our ears. They were empty.

I asked Vernon to inventory everything liquid we had, including the champagne and to let me know what it amounted to. I went to the chart table and got out my dividers. I set them at one hundred eighty miles and stepped off the distance home on the chart. We were just under 900 miles from Honolulu. It would take about five days to get there if we maintained an average of 180 miles per day.

Vernon reported back that, including champagne, we had just over seven gallons of potable liquid on hand.

I asked him to work out a ration at the rate of one gallon per day for the entire crew and institute it. We had to keep some water in reserve. We couldn't count on an average of 180 miles per day, nor could we be sure no other disaster would befall us, slowing us further. I asked him to work out a new menu. We could use no more dehydrated food. I reminded him to see that no juices were lost from canned fruits and vegetables. They would make a good supplement to our water ration. He, of course, didn't need reminding, but I felt it best that every helpful thought be spoken.

Before our departure, we had discussed water stores and the assumption generally was that the required amount was more than ample. At one of our meetings with the race committee, an official had said, and I quote: "I know some of you guys are going to start pumping water over the side as soon as you round Catalina in order to cut weight, but the rule requires 15 gallons per man. See that you have it aboard."

We had put it aboard, and had not pumped it over the side.

Discussing the situation, to find some reason for our dry starboard tank, Vernon expressed a belief that the tank must have a leak. Joe, however, was convinced that our dehydrated menu was at fault and that we had just used it up too fast. This didn't, however, explain the shortage in one tank only.

I am sure the tanks were full when we started. I checked them myself. We arrived at no conclusion at this time, but this is what I believe happened:

First, the two tanks are connected by a short hose. There is a "cut-off" valve between them. I believe this valve was not closed tightly and as we pumped water from the port tank, heeled over as we were, the water from the higher starboard tank drained back into the one to port.

I didn't question the crew regarding their use of water. It would serve no purpose now, but I do believe we used a considerable amount in our cooking, and further, that we had been a bit too free with it in other uses. We would pay for that freedom from now on.

As I remember, our dinner that night consisted of corned beef hash, stewed tomatoes and melba toast. The toast was dry and powdery in my mouth, but the tomatoes were juicy and good. We were each allowed two-thirds of a glass of fluid in any form we wanted it mixed, milk, punch or coffee.

I wanted the champagne used early. It wouldn't be fair to non-drinkers to leave it until last. It took four of us, however, to split a bottle at the agreed ration and I had no takers that night when I suggested it.

It was a rather serious, quiet group gathered around the cockpit and galley as night fell and regular watches were re-established.

I had also noticed something else that continued to disturb me. As I had been on the helm that evening I detected a small amount of play in the wheel. I had a wrench brought and tightened it as much as I could, but the play persisted. After I was relieved at the wheel, I took a flashlight and crawled back under the cockpit. I examined the steering system from end to end but could find nothing amiss. As I emerged, Jorge and Kevin were in the cabin taping red plastic over a flashlight, readying it for use in lighting the compass. Jorge looked at me and asked: "How are things under there?"

"Just checking," I answered. I didn't want to mention the slipping if I could avoid it. I felt the crew had quite enough for one day. I was also, I'm afraid, holding to that old practice of facing problems: "Don't notice it, and maybe it will go away."

CHAPTER IX

As I entered the cockpit some hours later, I found I would have to face the new problem whether I wanted to or not. Vernon said: "Stu I think you'd better take the wheel for awhile. It feels like it's slipping now and then."

Still hoping I could ignore it, I answered: "I've just checked the whole system, and it's tight and intact. I thought I noticed something too, but it must be just the way the sea is flowing around the rudder that makes it feel that way."

When I thought back over what I had said, it sounded very weak indeed. I'm sure I convinced no one, including myself.

I went below, opened the compartment under the cockpit and got out the emergency tiller and a wrench. I placed them in the cockpit and suggested this might be a better place to have them from now on.

The "sound box" that was my bunk produced a new grinding noise that night. I was awake for some time trying to sort it out in my mind. I mentally went completely through the steering system again. Trying to determine what could produce this particular sound.

My check of the system earlier had not included the chain and sprocket up in the steering post under the compass. It must be coming from there, I thought. We'll dissemble that in the morning and see what we find.

Later, after the watch change, I heard Joe crawling around under the cockpit floor. I got up and joined him when he crawled out. He had checked the system as I had and come up with the same finding—nothing. We agreed it must be in the steering column, but, so long as it didn't get worse, we could leave an examination of that area until morning. We had best, however, reduce the load on the rudder as much as we could. We went on deck and doused the mainsail for the night. The twin headsails did cause Anuenue to wander from side to side a bit, but she corrected with little pressure on the rudder.

In the morning, the wind was down some. We weren't moving well, but the first order of business was an examination of the rest of the steering system to see if we could find the cause of the play in the wheel. We brought up tools, and removed the compass; the sprocket, mounted on the steering wheel shaft, was just under it. Joe and I observed while Vernon was on the wheel. He, Vernon, would call out:

"Now" when he felt the wheel slip. Joe and I, watching, saw nothing amiss. Anuenue was beautiful, but she could be a frustrating mistress. Feminine to the end, I thought.

We finally gave it up and reset the compass in its mounting. There was nothing we could find wrong with the steering system.

I got out my sextant and shot the sun as it climbed slowly up the sky behind us. When I had computed the line, and corrected back to eight o'clock, I found we had covered just one hundred and seventy miles in the twenty-four hours from 8 a.m. July 12th to 8 a.m. July 13th, which was discouraging indeed. We sat for awhile, Vernon, Joe, and I puzzling over the steering problem. We concluded it had to be outside the hull, and this meant the blade of the rudder was slipping on the post. The rudder blade was made of high density foam molded over a steel framework that was welded to the rudder post. Our conclusion was that the foam must have compressed from the tremendous pressures to which it had been subjected, and separated from the framework enough to allow the framework to slip in the blade.

We considered installing the spare wooden rudder I had made for just such an eventuality. It was considerably smaller, however, and from the experience we had to date, we feared we would have to reduce sail even further to be able to steer with it.

We were still in a race, and wanted to cross the finish line as soon as possible. The use of a spinnaker, however, was out of the question in our present condition.

We were meandering from side to side under the twins, requiring constant rudder correction. We concluded we would be just as well off with the main back up. This would increase the pressure a bit, but it would keep it on one side, for the most part, and make for less wear upon the rudder. Back up went the mainsail, and I set a course to keep the wind from the starboard quarter. Our heading was just over 260 degrees magnetic, well north of the Islands.

During the morning, as the sun rose higher and higher in the sky, the temperature rose with it, and the water problem began monopolizing our attention. I heard Vernon at one time verbally chastising his boys for complaining of thirst. When we were alone in the cockpit together later, I brought up the subject, suggesting that the mere knowledge that water was scarce would increase the desire for it. I said I, too, came off the wheel now with a parched throat, and that I didn't remember it being the same when water was plentiful. It was happening to all of us, Vernon said. Most of the crew had mentioned thirst to him in one way or another.

Later in the morning, as I saw another rainbow reflected back to us from a "squall" ahead, I remember the one of the day before, and suddenly I knew where the good fortune was. I looked back up the wind line. There were other squalls there; not as many as the day before, but several that should pass over, or near us.

I went below and came back up with our mainsail cover. I called Kevin and Craig to give me a hand and we spread the wide part of the cover out over the cabin top with the narrower portion reaching back into the cockpit. We fastened it here and there until we had fashioned a large canvas bowl with a trough down into the cockpit. At the end of the trough we collected our buckets and waited.

As the nearest squall approached, it appeared as though it would pass to our right, so I ordered the helm up a bit to put us in its line.

Excitement was growing. Everyone was getting into the act. There were hands all around the sail cover to help guide the water into the buckets.

The squall came by. We were just in the edge of it and the rain began. Before the canvas was more than wet, the squall had passed and the rain stopped. Craig went below and brought up a saucer. He began scraping the wet canvas toward the trough and the bucket. We collected about a half cup of water. I tasted it and passed it around. It tasted of canvas, but it was fresh and good regardless.

Joe, who was at the helm, said: "You guys should have seen what poured off the mainsail out at the end of the boom while you were collecting that drop."

I looked at the end of the boom. It was still dripping heavily.

"It should be good," Joe continued, "the sail was pretty well washed in the rain yesterday."

I went forward and toyed with the "Satori Reef'. When I pulled it in just a little, there was a large well-formed trough at the bottom of the sail running down and out to the end of the boom. I hauled the reef all the way in to ascertain if I could lift the end of the boom enough to cause the incline to reverse and run the water toward the mast. But the sail flattened too much and the heel of the boat was too great anyway. We would just have to devise means of collecting the run-off from the outer end.

I returned to the cockpit and asked the crew to haul in the boom. They did, and I snapped a block with a light line through it to the boom bail. The boom was run out as I played out the line. When it was back in position, I lashed a bucket to the two ends of the line and pulled it out to the boom end. It hung there beautifully, right under the clew of the sail.

We were all watching intently as the bucket swung there when a wave, larger than its companions, lifted Anuenue's quarter and the boom dipped. The bucket hit the sea, bounced up and struck again. When the sea had passed and the boom came up, the bucket was overflowing with salt water.

"Back to the drawing board," I said, and hauled the bucket back into the cockpit.

One of the boys went below and came back up with the boat hook. It was the aluminum extension type and, fully extended, reached easily to the end of the boom. We lashed the bucket to its end and reached it out. We found we could nest it in the boom bail, and when the boat heeled, draw it back quickly to keep it out of the sea.

This should do it. Now for another squall. We looked around, but there were none in our area, so we collapsed the boat hook and placed it in the cockpit, handy for use when one came along.

Time of "local" noon was approaching, so I got out my navigation tools in readiness for a latitude shot.

My watch had not been keeping good time, but I had set it to Greenwich Mean Time and was using it anyway. I couldn't keep up with the changes Vernon and Joe were making with their watch settings as they were correcting from Pacific Daylight Savings Time to Hawaiian Time. I checked mine several times a day by radio and made corrections for its error as required.

When I had completed my latitude shot, I found we had moved well north. We were within 30 miles of the rhumb line from L. A. to Honolulu.

Morning weather charts were still showing a nice picture of the weather back along the Pacific Coast which interested us not one bit. We had picked up one report from Honolulu that indicated a high, a couple of hundred miles northeast of the Islands. We had no details concerning it, but our present course would take us quite close to the position where we had plotted it, and a windless waste was something we could do without.

We unwound our spiderweb shortly after noon, jibed over onto port tack and rewoved the web. Our new course with the sails trimmed was 235 degrees magnetic, heading us right toward the "Big Island" of Hawaii at the southern end of the island chain. We were still almost 700 miles out.

We sailed on through the afternoon with a real weather eye over the stern watching for a nice plump squall to come along. I went down for a nap, and when I came up, Craig had made improvements on our water collecting device. He had lashed a wooden coat hanger to the end of the boat hook with the curved arm reaching out beyond the bucket and down. Resting the coat hanger on the main sheets, one could slide the bucket out to its position under the boom end and back to the cockpit with the greatest of ease. Later in the afternoon, we had a chance to try it when a small squall crossed over us. We worked frantically while the rain lasted, not waiting for the bucket to fill, but bringing it in frequently and emptying it to avoid the risk of dipping it into the sea.

The water was good, there wasn't a hint of salt in it. We each had a good deep swallow and put two quarts into storage.

Spirits were high that evening. Gordo, who had not been feeling well and was relieved from watch duty, prepared canned beans and fruit for dinner. He, Joe, Jorge and I split a bottle of champagne for our liquid ration. We were really living it up—beans and champagne— who could ask for more?

News from Honolulu via radio that evening reported *Windward Passage* and *Blackfin* over the line and finished. It was Sunday, and the spectator fleet was reported to be enormous as they battled down the Molokai (Kaiwi) Channel. Other contenders were closing in, and we were clearly out of the running unless our move south paid off. We still couldn't risk a chute with our rudder continuing to act up. It did continue, at times there was a full spoke (about 8 inches) play in the wheel. We hadn't given up the race however. We continued to "squeeze" for the wind to hold as we moved south, and for it to let up over the rest of the fleet to the north.

Such is yacht racing.

N
41
29100

CHAPTER X

I was finding real satisfaction in navigating. I had signed Joe on originally as my right hand sailing the boat, and as navigator. From the first, however, he was kept so busy tending to mechanical problems that there was no time left to him for "star gazing". He was a first-rate shipmate and a "top sailor". I don't know what we'd have done without him, but I was pleased, for my own selfish reasons, that we hadn't left him time to navigate.

There was a certain "fulfillment", hard to describe, in shooting a sight with the sextant, working through the computations and coming up with a position line that you knew was correct. There was a "sameness" about the ocean most of the way down, after the first few days of solid overcast. The sky was five to nine-tenths covered with clouds most of the time. The winds ranged between twelve and eighteen knots, except for the start and finish. The seas changed relatively little. There were only three real "places" out there: the center of a circle of the ocean that was us, the place where the sun rose off our stern, and the place where the sun set, fine off the starboard bow; yet when I shot my sights and got a fix, the ocean about us looked, and felt, like where we were.

As we moved south and west throughout the night of the 13th, the ocean and the air about us did change. Even though the wind stayed up, there was a balmy feeling in the air and seeping down into the cabin.

There was also a fascinating new noise back in my bunk to be sorted out and analyzed. We were on a port run now, and this required the use of the starboard winch in trimming the genny sheet. It was located just above and outboard of my head when I slept. The first time the crew trimmed the sheet, I awoke with the clicking of the palls in the winch as they ground away. The clicking stopped; the crew was obviously cleating down the sheet. Then I heard a "tong" in a low key. It's the line stretching around the winch, I thought, and then "tang", a higher note, not a "third" or a "fifth" as a next note up a chord should be, but somewhere in between, leaving another yet to be anticipated. It came -- "ting", well up the scale -- but still unresolved. I waited, there had to be one more note, but it didn't come. I was left unresolved, suspended in anticipation. Each time the sail setting was changed it was the same. The sheet would stretch with its "tong", "tang", "ting", never completing a chord.

From my other side, somewhere deep within the hull, came the grinding noise that had not as yet been identified.

What was it?

Would it rain tomorrow?

When would the sheet stretch again?

I finally went to sleep.

I awoke a couple of hours later and climbed out into a cockpit wet with rain. Kevin called excitedly:

"Hey, Stu, we got four gallons of water."

It was true, they had. A beauty of a squall had come along and drenched them. The new water collection system had functioned perfectly, and our water supply was now better than when we had discovered the shortage. This called for a celebration, so Vernon and I went below and brewed a cup of coffee. It was Oh! so good. The crew on watch had drunk their fill already, and there would be extra rations for the others when they awoke.

One of our problems was being overcome. Now if we could only find a solution to the other one. Vernon reported no improvement in the wheel, however; it was still slipping erratically—sometimes just a little, sometimes a full spoke.

In the morning, I would go through the system again. Maybe it was inside somewhere and we were just missing it. I thought again of the spare rudder, but again rejected the idea of a change now. Our speed was still holding up well, and it would cost us a couple of hours at least to make the change. That was fifteen miles and I didn't want to give it away. We would wait until the rudder dropped off, and then install the spare.

• • •

The morning roll call reported more "A" boats across the finish line, and the leading "B's" closing in. *Americana* was still out ahead of us and somewhat north. *Curioso*, as expected, passed her call, and there was still no report from *Hawaiiana*.

I shot a morning sun line, but didn't attempt to compute an 8 a.m. position. I had switched to a noon plot the day before. At noon today, we would be ten days out of Los Angeles, and an examination of the chart indicated we would be approximately five hundred miles from home. Our target had been to arrive on the twelfth day. A study of past race results had indicated it would have to be then, if we were to be in contention. We wouldn't do it obviously. It was disheartening to have had this opportunity of a lifetime and then be unable to compete.

I suffered a number of pangs of this type those last few days—self pity, I presume—but I was able to shake them off. I had a boat to get across the finish line, winner or "also ran".

• • •

We sustained our first injury that morning when someone, I don't remember who, a bit overcome with fatigue no doubt, let Anuenue have her head and the main boom jibed across with a bang. Vernon had crawled back into my bunk for an off-duty snooze, and as the traveler struck the stop over his head, he sat up quickly with a start, not remembering he had no head room. He crawled out dazed, and with blood streaming down his face. He had really clouted himself. Jorge was summoned, and he came quickly with his medical kit, pleased I am sure to have a real live patient to work on. He did a neat job. He cleaned Vernon up, stopped the bleeding with pressure and closed the gash with an adhesive tape butterfly patch. He called me to admire his handiwork before he closed it over with a bandage.

"Beautiful," I said.

Vernon did look the "old salt" now—two weeks of white stubble on his face and a patch on his head did something for him.

We kept him down for the morning, but he was back up and operating by lunchtime. We kidded him a bit—our only injury, and in bed, yet! He took it with grace.

As "local noon" approached, I tied myself standing in the cockpit and shot the sun. We were down to latitude 23 degrees north. And after advancing the morning sun line a distance equal to our estimated morning's run, I marked our noon position at four hundred and eighty miles from Diamond Head. Just under one hundred and eighty miles run since yesterday, I noted.

As we sailed on to the southeast through the afternoon, our surroundings took on more and more of the feel of home. The squalls, still dotting the horizon around us, were smaller and not so gray and dark as they had been a few days before. The sea and the sky were lighter and bluer. We were all in shorts now, even at night, and the ones with a sun-resistant skin were shirtless most of the day. Sleeping bags and blankets had been folded and stacked on the unused upper starboard bunk. Foul weather gear was a thing of the past. My oilskin pants which had ripped out in the seat, went over the side along with some of the over-used clothing of my shipmates.

The wind held, the seas stayed up and we even surfed occasionally as the afternoon passed. This tack could still be a right choice, I thought. Maybe the wind is letting down further north.

It was a wistful, wishful thought.

As dawn of the 15th brightened into day, the wind began to ease and the seas began to flatten. By mid-morning we were down to around five knots, gliding along like any Sunday sailor. When the knot meter dropped to four, I gave up squeezing for more wind and went to my bunk for some needed sleep.

It was relatively quiet when I crawled in. The flow of water along the hull produced only a faint gurgle.

I awoke an hour later, rubbed the sleep from my eyes and listened intently. That gurgle was louder. There was even a reasonable slap on the hull now and then. I scrambled out, climbed to the cockpit and looked at the knotmeter. It registered between six and six and a half knots. Great, I thought. All is not lost. Jorge was on the helm as I walked back to look at the compass. I'm sure my eyes bugged as I saw it. He was steering 210 degrees.

"Where are you going, man?" I cried. "Tahiti?"

"I'm just keeping the wind on the quarter," he replied, "like we have been."

He was right. I had left no instructions to be followed in the event of a wind shift, and this was a shift I might have anticipated. I was getting a bit fatigued and careless I decided. I'd have to pay a little more attention.

There was enough crew awake to jibe in these relatively calm conditions, so I took the wheel and set them to the task. We unwound our web and wound it up on the other side. My noon latitude fix, taken a few moments later, placed us down to the latitude of Honolulu at 21 degrees 20 minutes. When I brought forward the morning line, I found we had covered one hundred eighty-seven miles in the past day. Not bad, I thought, considering the mileage we had lost in the light air that morning.

We were due east of Honolulu, three hundred and twenty miles out. Our new heading home was 259 degrees magnetic. We were making just north of that and keeping our fore quadrilateral filled.

I had gone back on the helm when Kevin, for some reason, pulled open the hatch to the under cockpit compartment. His head popped up, his eyes wide. He said: "Stu, I just saw a bolt head move."

Joe was stirring in the cabin behind him.

I called: "Joe, take a look."

Joe was already on the way.

They disappeared under the cockpit for some time.

I heard Joe call for something and as Kevin reappeared, I asked: "What'd he say? What'd he say?"

Kevin answered: “He wants some tape. I’m getting it for him.”

The next few moments took forever to pass. Finally Joe crawled out, closed the hatch and climbed into the cockpit with a faint smile on his face. He sat down and said: “It’s the bolt through the quadrant and the rudder shaft. It’s sheared.”

“Sheared,” I exclaimed. “That’s half-inch stainless steel.”

“Nevertheless,” Joe continued, “it’s sheared. When the pressure was off, I could lift each piece out of the hole with my fingers.”

“Will it hold?” I asked.

“It’ll hold,” Joe answered. “We’ve probably elongated the hole in the quadrant and we’ll continue to have play in the wheel, but it can’t go anywhere. I taped the pieces in place.”

“How about the chute?” I asked.

“Let’s put it up,” Joe answered.

The crew had gathered around to listen to Joe’s explanation of what he had found.

I looked up and said: “Go! The three-quarter ounce.”

They were off, and so was Anuenue, from six knots to eight and a half as soon as the spinnaker was up and drawing.

We would at least avoid the distinction of winning the “tail-end Charlie” trophy.

It was a gorgeous sail that afternoon. The wind built up to about ten to fifteen knots and was higher in the squalls. We were able to hold her in the flatter seas, if we got her running off as a squall line passed, but she still rounded up occasionally. I switched to the 1.5 ounce chute. I didn't want to blow out the light one. The wind might go down again and we would need it.

When I awoke from a nap later, Jorge greeted me with; "Hey, Skipper, we've been talking, and we've decided we can fly the chute all the way in."

I answered: "What do you mean—you've decided? I made that decision when it went up."

Everyone was pleased, and the excitement was growing as we closed slowly on the Island chain that was home.

I set up a schedule for the night that would include Vernon and Craig as helmsmen. Five of us would stand half-hour watches in rotation. Jorge and Gordo announced they didn't need much sleep and volunteered their services throughout the night helping in the cockpit and keeping the coffee water hot. We had almost forgotten our water shortage. There were squalls regularly, and we could pick up our needs from the heavens almost at will.

We had champagne and beans for dinner again. It was time for celebrations; after all, I told them: "If it's clear, we may sight land in the morning."

This comment was a mistake, I learned later. It created an expectation that was not likely to be fulfilled. The Island of Hawaii was still a hundred miles away, off the port bow, and we were not likely to pass closer than sixty miles from it. Haleakala on Maui would be within thirty miles by mid-afternoon if we held our due westerly heading. It was ten thousand feet high, and we had a better chance of seeing that, but only if the squalls abated. These were so numerous that they formed a curtain around us only a few miles away.

The boys off watch had the radio tuned to a Honolulu station that was reporting the news. As the announcer finished with local news and turned to sports, we heard him mention the Transpac. Everyone quieted down to listen. A number of boats had crossed during the day, all of them Class "A" and "B". But, he reported, the leaders in Class "C" —*Argonaut* and *Quasar*— were approaching the Molokai channel and were expected to cross the finish line sometime around midnight.

I suggested we stop listening to tragedy and see if we could get some use out of that radio direction finder.

Jorge turned the band selector knob and tuned in on Makapuu. Its "daa, daa, dit, dit" came in clear and strong. He swung the directional antenna back and forth a bit and turned down the volume to better find the null. Makapuu was almost dead ahead. If off at all, it was slightly to port. I plotted it three degrees from that.

"Now," I said, "let's see if we can find a Hilo station."

Jorge switched back to standard broadcast and began listening to stations up and down the dial. It took some time, but finally an announcer identified his location as Hilo, Hawaii. We labeled the spot on the dial with masking tape and started swinging the directional antenna. Hilo was on a bearing of just over 210 degrees magnetic, still well ahead of abeam. I plotted the line and circled the "X" where it crossed the line from Makapuu. We were creeping a little north of our course, I noted. I cautioned the helmsmen to hold as close to the 260 degree heading as they could, and to be sure and report their best judgment of the course made good.

I hoped I was hiding the symptoms, but if the truth were known, it would be that I was becoming a bit tensed up about my first landfall. I must guard against conveying this, I thought; it wouldn't be good for crew moralc.

I couldn't keep it from myself, however. I finished an early stint at the helm that night and then tried to sleep, but sleep just wouldn't come. Finally, only a few minutes before I was due to go on watch again, I became so sleepy I couldn't hold my head up. I felt mortified, but I had to pass my turn at the wheel. Up until this time I had always been able to awaken completely whenever the need required that I be awake. Not so this time: I would put the boat and crew in jeopardy, I thought, if I didn't pass. Kevin followed me on watch, and he took the early duty in good spirits. I crawled back in my bunk and passed out.

Gordo was on steward duty when I awoke, and he was right on hand with a hot cup of coffee and some dry wit. His malaise had passed, and he was himself again.

Joe had just come off duty and reported that the wind had backed a little further to the east and that we were having to hold at around 270 degrees to 275 degrees to keep from sailing by the lee.

This will put us further from Hawaii and Maui, I thought, and make a sighting by day less likely. It would certainly be nice for one of those mountains to pop up over the horizon, visual bearings were easy to take, and we could establish a position, exactly, before our run in.

With morning, the wind lightened and we were back to the three-quarter ounce chute. We still moved well, but the seas remained relatively flat and there was little surfing to be enjoyed. The knotmeter stayed between seven and eight knots.

Morning news from Honolulu listed boats by the dozen across the finish. *Argonaut* had crossed around one a.m. and was apparently first over-all as well as first in Class “C”. We were just under 200 miles out.

My crew kept searching the southern horizon all morning long. I too kept looking for one of those mountains to show itself, but the cloud curtain hung to the ocean without a gap. By 11 a.m. I decided it was time to jibe and move a little closer in. Our course throughout the night had continued to take us a little north of a direct line to Diamond Head and thus a little further from Hawaii and Maui. We jibed to port, and as noon approached, I went below to gather my navigational tools for a latitude fix. This one had to be good, I thought. The test is coming up soon.

As I started back out to the cockpit, Vernon stopped me to talk about something. I don’t remember now what the subject was, but he wanted my attention and I gave it to him. When I got to the cockpit, I lashed myself upright, zeroed my sextant in on the sun, brought it down to the horizon and held it there. I watched for a moment, and to my surprise and anguish, saw the sun sinking slowly into the horizon. Noon had passed. I had missed my shot. I had to consciously control my annoyance with Vernon for having stopped me for conversation.

It wasn't, of course, all that important. I had merely turned into a bundle of nerves with concern over my landfall and was having a hard time hiding it.

I went below and computed a line from what I had. It crossed the morning line at a good angle and gave me a reliable fix, but my pique with myself for allowing this to happen continued throughout the afternoon.

I was still confident that I knew where I was. I could "feel it". But a visual sign would be reassuring. My computation had put us twenty-five miles north of the direct line I had drawn to Diamond Head. It was no wonder we hadn't seen mountains beyond the curtain of clouds. A compass course of 256 degrees magnetic would now take us directly home. I took out my large scale chart of the Islands, taped it down over the Pacific chart and transferred the noon position.

The Transpac communications instructions called for a report to Honolulu by radio when two hundred miles out. We had passed this point during the night before and were now 140 miles from the finish line. The boys had been urging me for some time to try a call, but I hadn't wanted to risk our last bit of battery power fruitlessly. They were urging again now, so I relented. "Just one call," I said. "If they don't answer, we wait."

Joe hooked up the batteries and checked the voltmeter.

"Still in the red," he said, "but there may be enough in them."

I turned on the set and waited for it to warm. The indicator light remained dark.

I rechecked communications instructions for the proper procedure, and pressed the "mike" button: "KWF, KWF, KWF, this is Anuenue. Do you read me? Over."

I released the button and a voice boomed back:

"This is KWF. We read you loud and clear Anuenue. Good to hear from you. Over."

"We've had battery problems. Weren't sure we could reach you," I said. "We're one hundred and forty miles out and will be in by noon tomorrow."

He reminded me to report again in the morning and we signed off.

A great sigh of relief went through the boat; it was good to be in contact with home.

We continued taking radio bearings throughout the afternoon. Makapuu was on the nose now and Hilo was abeam. We located KMVI on Maui and marked it on the dial. It moved slowly back as did Hilo while the day of the 16th faded into evening.

The crew had been working me over all afternoon. When I had reported only one hundred eighty-five miles for the day's run at noon, they didn't want to believe it: "Honest, we had the chute up constantly. Haven't we been moving well most of the time?" they argued.

"Yes, we have," I agreed, "but we haven't surfed in flat seas and the wind was light most of the morning," I reminded them.

I think they meant it. Vernon even suggested I recheck my figures. "It would be futile," I told him. I had shot several sunlines during the afternoon, and they all lined up with our knotmeter at about seven and a half knots.

I checked out for another much needed nap, and when I awoke and crawled out of my sack, I was puzzled by the activity that Joe and Jorge were engaged in.

They had a piece of blue cotton yardage. They were measuring it very carefully, marking it lengthwise with a pencil and cutting it in long narrow strips. When they finished marking and cutting, they began picking up the ends and stapling them together.

I watched with interest and wonder—my curiosity growing. Finally I could wonder no longer. I asked, "What in the world are you guys up to?"

Jorge answered with a question: "Didn't you say you wanted a going home pennant?"

"We are making one," said Joe.

I had expressed a wish for just such a pennant and had described one some time before we left. Joe and Jorge had gone out and bought the cloth and they were now making a "Going Home" pennant in the old battleship tradition. It would be perfect for our homecoming. I was more than pleased.

• • •

We had grown so accustomed to emergencies of one type or another, that the one most fearful danger at sea hardly disturbed our normal routine of activity, when it presented itself. Gordo was preparing dinner this last evening out when suddenly fire covered the whole galley corner of the cabin where the stove was located. Flames rose to the cabin ceiling, and ran like a waterfall down the front face of the oven onto the deck below. I was at the wheel watching. Gordo calmly picked up a blanket and covered the whole unit, down to the deck. The flame was gone, and the moment for excitement was over before it got well started. The pressure was gone from the alcohol tank by now, so Craig opened the hatch in the cockpit where it was located and started pumping. Gordo called immediately for him to stop. Alcohol was spurting from a fractured fitting next to one of the burners. We mopped up the fuel, closed down the stove for the evening, and settled for corned beef out of a can. No one was really concerned about a cold dinner this night; we would have steaks tomorrow.

• • •

Later, after dinner, the radio was switched to Honolulu for the six o'clock news reports. Our island competitors were in the news. *Curioso* had crossed in the morning. First Hawaiian boat in. *Hawaiiana* had crossed a little after 4 p.m. and *Americana* was in the channel.

As darkness fell, Craig reported that he thought he saw a flash of light off on the horizon to our left. We all peered intently for some time but we saw nothing.

At eight o'clock, I went below and took another round of bearings with the RDF, working with the radio for some time. I advanced our position from my last sunline to account for the estimated miles run and it checked well with the RDF.

Everyone was awake. This was no night for sleeping.

I called the helmsmen together to make my commitment on landfall.

"You should see a light," I said, "about midnight, thirty degrees off the port bow. That will be the light on the tip of Kalaupapa, Molokai. Be on the lookout for it. If I'm asleep, wake me."

They would be alert, I was sure. Now, at nine o'clock, I went down for a nap. I was awakened an hour later. Kevin was shaking my foot. As I emerged from my bunk, he said: "Come Stu, we've got lights, and we've got traffic!"

He was bubbling over with excitement.

I stepped into the cockpit, ducked out from under the dodger and looked to port.

There on the horizon, like two nuggets nestled in cotton and not a hands-width apart, were the lights of two small towns casting a golden glow on the overhanging clouds. Another hands-width to the left a rotating beacon slashed the sky with its beam as it turned through our quadrant every few seconds.

It wasn't a matter of time. I recognized the scene immediately.

I had raised a family from grade school to marriage just toward the sunrise from that beacon. My two boys with their families would be not far from there now.

I had built *Dee Jay*, my first little cruising ketch, and later *Geisha*, my sleek Thunderbird sloop, within a mile of the airport the beacon lighted. Both boats had been launched and sailed from the harbor adjacent to the glowing town on the left. There were many friends and treasured memories sleeping there. They flashed back through my mind in clear relief as I stood there gazing.

Along those beaches not too long ago I had......

"Well, what is it?" Kevin asked, interrupting my reverie.

"That rotating light is the Maui Airport. The towns are Kahului and Wailuku," I answered.

We were some thirty miles out, and I had not anticipated seeing them.

Joe was already taking bearings over the compass.

I looked around for the traffic. There was a steamer off in the distance astern, still several miles away. Off our port bow, also some distance away were the lights of another vessel I couldn't identify. As I looked at it, I noticed dimly in the distance beyond another rotating beacon flashing against the low hanging clouds.

"That will be the Molokai Airport, Joe," I called. "Get a cross bearing on it."

Kevin was standing by watching the proceedings as though he had personally discovered land and was overjoyed with his find. "Where does your navigation put us, Stu?" he asked.

"Give me your course and speed over the last few hours and I'll plot it," I answered.

He gave me his estimates, and I went below to the chart table to measure it off from my last fix. I made an "X".

"There," I said.

Joe called down the bearings he had taken and I plotted them. They crossed at the exact longitude of my "X" and four miles south.

"How's that?" I asked, "considering I didn't get a latitude shot today."

"Not bad," said Kevin. He was grinning all over.

The crew was wide awake now, and would stay awake until we were home.

It was a long, slow night from that point on. Out on the Pacific, with nothing but the stars to watch as they rose, made their turn through the heavens and set. The sound of our bow wave could convince us we were making tremendous speed as we sailed along through the night; but, with the lights on shore to measure our progress by and home just across the horizon, our movement was like a snail's pace.

The Kalaupapa light was in view two points off the port bow soon after midnight.

Joe and I continued to clutter my chart with bearing lines throughout the night as new reference points were observed and identified.

We still had a boat to sail, however, and the watch schedule had to be maintained. The winds continued light and fair, as Joe's watch wore into Craig's, Craig's into Kevin's, and Kevin's into

Vernon's. That close to the finish was when we took our worst knockdown of the trip. The steamer I had spotted first was within a quarter of a mile behind us when I noticed a black cloud hanging low and blotting out the stars astern. Vernon was at the helm as the squall began slapping at us with its advance gusts. I was supposed to be the experienced helmsman, so he slid out from behind the wheel and I slid in. The squall hit us with its main body, and we were over on our ear within seconds. I needn't have relieved Vernon, I thought; he could have performed this feat fully as well as I.

The crewmen who had been resting below came scrambling out on deck as they felt Anuenue go over. Jorge headed for the foredeck. I called below for the spreader lights to be turned on; the batteries may be almost dead, I thought, but they would just have to take the drain. As the switch was thrown, they flooded the deck with light; tired as the batteries might be they served us well at this particular moment.

The crew had been exceptionally neat during the day, preparing for their homecoming, while tidying up lines in ship-shape order. The spinnaker halyard was coiled and secured with a loop pulled through and doubled back over the coil. It tangled badly, however, as Jorge worked frantically to clear it. My call to hurry didn't help, I'm sure, but I was concerned about the chute. It was the three-quarter ounce and the way it whipped and snapped off to leeward, it sounded as if it were beating itself to shreds. Jorge worked and worked but the tangle wouldn't let go. I was becoming concerned about the chute, so I called for a knife. A mere touch was all that was necessary, that did it. The halyard let go with a resounding "twang" and the chute came down in the sea. The boys hauled it in while I, watching them and not watching the wind, let the main boom bang back and forth several times before the squall was done with us and passed on.

Within fifteen minutes from the start of this episode the wind was back down to a gentle breeze of eight to ten knots. I left the chute down until dawn, however, it was too late in the race to have it torn apart by a temperamental squall coming out of nowhere with little warning.

We reset the twin head sails and turned off the spreader lights.

I looked back. The steamer was still there, a quarter of a mile astern.

She had apparently hove to in order to watch the wild flapping thing on the sea ahead of her. I wondered about the language that might have been spoken by her crew on watch. They were likely to have been displeased to have been held up this way by "mad" sailors floundering around wildly in the middle of the night, and in the middle of the sea lanes.

After we had calmed Anuenue and had her moving again, we settled down to our plotting, and I discovered that all of a sudden I had become land shy. Joe and I spent the rest of the night taking bearings. He kept assuring me that we were well offshore, and our plots confirmed this. I continued to be concerned, however, about running in on the dark western tip of Molokai. The night was black and we could see nothing of this dark end of the Island. A faint glow had appeared, however, low in the sky ahead. It took me some time to identify it. I finally pointed it out to Joe as I had been steering by it for some time. I said: "Joe, that must be Honolulu."

After he had taken a long look he agreed: "It must be."

This night was almost endless, but dawn finally came and Joe had been right. When we could see, we discovered we were a good seven to eight miles off Molokai and entering the Channel.

We put the three-quarter ounce chute back up with first light. It was none the worse for its beating of the night just past.

After a breakfast of canned fruit, (there wasn't a drop of water left for coffee), I started preparing for our homecoming. I went below, stripped and returned to the cockpit with a bucket and a bottle of liquid "Joy". I dipped water from the sea and calmly bathed myself in the cockpit while Gordo ground away with the movie camera. While rinsing, I sustained our second injury and gave Jorge his second opportunity to "come to the fore". I threw a bucket over the side on a line for rinse water. It filled and drew astern before I started to retrieve it. As the line came taut, it dragged my arm along the stern pulpit rubbing off several square inches of skin in the process. Jorge arose to the occasion. He had another patch job to do, and he did it neatly and with dispatch.

I finished my toiletry by shaving my two weeks' growth of stubble down to sideburns and chin whiskers. That should be salty enough for them I thought as I checked myself in the mirror.

I returned to the cockpit neatly dressed in white shorts, my "Anuenue" shirt and white "Topsider" shoes.

The rest of the crew, feeling the warmth of home approaching, had begun going through the same process.

At the helm, the compass was no longer necessary; Makapuu was there -- big, clear, and solid -- fine on the starboard bow. Our passage toward it down the Channel was relatively smooth in the gentle weather, but the helm still took a bit of man-handling now and then.

As we drew nearer to Oahu, Craig began to urge me to place the second radio call. I held off.

"I don't want to sound like a novice," I said, "over-excited from my first sight of land."

Frankly, I had moments of wanting to sneak by the finish line unnoticed, particularly when I thought back to the finish I had conjured for myself before my departure for California.

I was finally forced to call however.

The receiver was on and we heard "Honolulu Transpac" in a ship-to-shore conversation discussing the probability of Anuenue showing up on the horizon soon. I could put it off no longer.

As we drew abeam of Koko Head, I called Kevin to the helm and went below to convey message to headquarters.

I turned on the set, let it warm up and pressed the mike button.

"Honolulu Transpac, this is Anuenue. Over," I said.

"This is Honolulu Transpac, come in Anuenue," a voice replied.

"We should be across by 10 a.m.," I said.

The voice came back with instructions to be on the lookout for a boat with "divers down" between us and the finish line. There was an underwater crew we were told, looking for the main mast *Mir* had lost a scant quarter mile from the Diamond Head finish line.

As we cleared Koko Head and entered the flat water beyond, my thoughts drifted back through the past thirteen days. If my story were told, I feared it would sound like "The Perils of Pauline" yet, beneath my feet was a stout ship. She had a steering problem, downwind in a seaway, yes. That could be corrected. She had a leak through her steering housing. This was later found to be the result of a careless workman's failure to put packing around the rudder shaft. She had, however, withstood a constant pounding—knock-downs and accidental jibes that should have cleared the spars from her decks a dozen times; but here she was as solid as a rock, having suffered no more damage to her rigging than a broken spinnaker car. She could be a winner, I thought, and she would be with a little loving care and attention.

Already she was acting the proverbial woman—putting on her best manners in preparation for meeting company. Her helm had eased down to the point where it required only an occasional tug to keep her heading for the finish line. I called Vernon and Joe to feel it. "You won't believe it," I said.

They didn't.

We passed the Kahala Hilton, and, from out of the morning sunrise there came the buzz of a light plane approaching us. I looked up and the glint of silver wings caught my eye. It circled and buzzed us, and circled again. We, of course, couldn't recognize the occupants, but I allowed as to how that was my daughter, Linda. Jorge agreed. She had planned to greet us in this fashion, and we were pretty sure she was carrying out her plan.

After a few buzzes, thc plane left; and we closed, in all our late splendor, on the finish line.

We crossed at 9:22 a.m., July 17th, last in class (of those who finished) and 54th in fleet standing. We were escorted to the finish by the press boat and met on the other side by a sleek cabin cruiser owned by my old friend "Dusty" Walker. Dusty was at the helm as he led us down off Waikiki, our spinnaker still flying, and then came alongside and told us to round up and douse. A tow was on the way, he said.

We doused the chute, but left the staysail and main up. We had one more duty to perform.

Joe and Jorge were on the foredeck. They had the boat hook lashed to the spinnaker halyard and all fifty-two feet of our "coming home" pennant attached to the end of it. Up it went, the boat hook standing well above the top of the mast. From its uppermost end, the pennant reached out and caught the blossom-scented breeze coming to us from off Waikiki. It undulated gently, off to leeward, as we drifted there —waiting.

Finally home.

EPILOG

It is September; the sports page reads:

"Newport 41's sweep Kahanamoku Series."

The three girls —*Americana*, *Hawaiiana*, and *Anuenue*— once stubborn, cantankerous women are now perfect ladies.

Mack McCutchen of Lindsey Plastics has been to Honolulu twice. On his second trip he brought three completely redesigned rudders and saw to their installation.

A spinnaker now is just another dress to be worn by the girls when their masters demand. And they wear them with elegance.

ABOUT THE AUTHOR

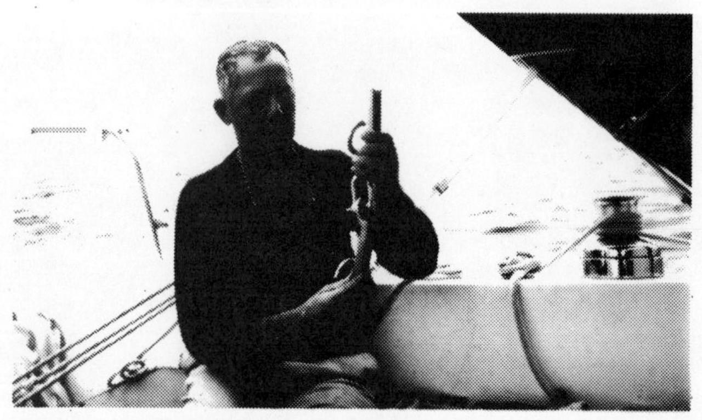

My Dad, John E. "Stu" Milligan was born in Muskogee, Oklahoma 1/7/13, but raised in Eugene, Oregon. One of 5 children, the son of a carpenter. Dad went to school in Eugene, and attended the University of Oregon.

Summer of 1933, fresh out of University of Oregon, he and a friend decided to go to Hawaii for the summer, and as Dad always said, "winter never came," so he never left.

Dad's first job in Hawaii was husking macadamia nuts, but he later graduated to a job managing a radio station in Shanghai in 1936, which he did until the Japanese invasion in '37, he was on the last ship leaving Shanghai.

He and my Mom, Daryl Jean Smith, were married in 1938, which was heralded by one of the strongest earthquakes to have hit Oahu!

Dad worked for California Packing Corp., and they moved to Molokai. The war years were tough on Molokai, but they kept busy, my two brothers were born on Molokai, I didn't come along till Dad was transferred back to Honolulu.

In 1949 they moved to Maui where Dad was Public and Industrial Relations Director for Hawaii Commercial and Sugar Company. Here they stayed until the family was grown.

During those years Dad built two sail boats in his backyard. The first was a salty ketch, short and squat, with baggy wrinkle on all her stays. Dad even melted the lead and poured his own keel. Later he bought Daryl a new sewing machine so HE could make all his own sails - her name was DeeJay (for my Mom). She was the first ocean going yacht off Maui, and the locals often called the Coast Guard to report that a boat was tipping over and was going to sink. They soon got used to Stu sailing off of Maalaea Harbor.

After moving into a new home, he started a new sailboat, the sleek, slender sloop, to be called Geisha (to represent the other woman in his life). She was a beauty, and when the time came for him to sell her, so he could realize his dream of sailing in the Transpac, his heart ached. The ad went in the paper, and who came to look, and eventually buy Geisha - A Col. Milligan, an air force officer, it was destiny. Although Dad took some razzing, when reports made it to the newspaper saying a boat named Geisha, captained by a man named Milligan had run hard aground off of Hickam Harbor!

Stu realized his dream and sailed in the 1969 Transpac and wrote of his experiences in "*The Rainbow Quest*", his boat —*Anuenue* (Hawaiian for Rainbow).

He was also in the State House Representatives from Maui in '58 and '60, ran for the first U. S. House of Representatives in '69, and was a member of the first Hawaii Public Employees Relations Board, appointed by then Governor John Burns and reappointed by Governor George Ariyoshi.

He retired in '83 and spent his remaining years in Hawaii Kai, where once again he decided to build a sailboat, a small one this time, just big enough to sail in the Hawaii Kai Marina waters, with a specially designed mast that he could collapse and sail under the bridges of the marina.

Other accomplishments in Dad's life include:

- flying a Sikorsky, he had his pilot's license till glaucoma impaired his sight.
- playing football for the University of Oregon, and later in Honolulu for the semi-pro "Town Team"
- an artist in many mediums, oil acrylics, and water colors
- and author of two previously published works (Cornell Maritime Press), *Celestial Navigation by H0249* which is still in publication, and another marine publication, *The Amateur Pilot*, which is now out of print.

Dad passed away in July of 1991, just 5 short months after Mom. They are scattered in ..."the wind, the sun, the salt of the sea..." they loved off of Oahu in Maunalua Bay.

Linda Milligan - Ugalde

W.E.C. Plant Publishing

Box 61751 Honolulu, Hawaii, 96839.
Voice: 808-622-0043 Fax: 808-622-1345
E-Mail: ALandJULIE.Plant@Worldnet.att.net

Current Books in Print

0-913611-03-4 *Radio's First Broadcaster* $9.95
by E. M. Plant 1990

Autobiography, Radio, Americana, Canadiana
Perfect Bound Trade Paperback, 104 pages

-Autobiography by a radio pioneer at the World's First Radio Station, 8MK (WWJ) Detroit Michigan 1919 to 1922.

The author recalls the early broadcasts of WWJ predated those of KDKA by several months. As 8MK the Detroit News transmitted daily under a public service licence from the Department of the Navy sharing the assigned frequency with Great Lakes steam ships.

0-913611-04-2 *Wahiawa Town - Hawaii Mini History* (series)
$3.95
by Al Plant illustrated by James Mercado 1995

Hawaii, History
Perfect Bound Trade Paperback, 32 pages

-This pocket sized book outlines the history of Honolulu County town where Dole began his pineapple empire at the turn of the 20th century. It documents the settlement from its first Polynesian settlers arrival in 700 Ad. until the end World War Two.

0-913611-05-0 *Gourmet Odyssey* $16.95
by Capt. Al and Julie Plant 1994

Boating, Cooking, Travel, Multicultural, Americana
Plastic Coil Bound Cloth, 196 pages

-Cooking in a yacht galley or tiny kitchen on a journey from Michigan to Molokai.

—A boating adventure cookbook of regional American recipes. The tale of a couple cruising from the Great Lakes to Florida via the Erie Canal, rivers, ocean and Intra-Coastal Waterway. Then their move to live and cook in the Pacific island paradise of Hawaii.

0-913611-06-9 *Petagwana to Pele, 3rd Edition* $12.95
by Al Plant 1994

Archaeology, Greatlakes, History
Perfect Bound Trade Paperback, 112 Pages

-The story of selected prehistoric and historic sites in the Detroit River region from Sarnia, Ontario\Port Huron, Michigan to Point Pelee, Ontario. A field guide for studying and visiting the featured archaeological sites.

0-913611-07-7 *Why? Boddah You?* $9.95
by James Mercado 1995

Cartoons, Hawaii, Multicultural, 124 pages
Perfect Bound Trade Paperback

-A collection of newspaper cartoons depicting Hawaii's lifestyle.

0-913611-08-5 *Write Fiction to Sell!* $16.95
by Joyce Brandon 1997

Writing Reference, Careers, How to,
8¼ x 5¼, Perfect Bound, 152 Pages, Acrylic Poly-Finish cover.

-Learn to weave the fictive dream by following the techniques demonstrated with examples from the author's own award-winning novels.